The Christian Mindset
In A Secular Society

The Christian Mindset In A Secular Society

Promoting Evangelical Renewal & National Righteousness

by
Carl F. H. Henry

MULTNOMAH PRESS
PORTLAND, OREGON 97266

Edited by Rod Morris
Cover design and illustration by Britt Taylor Collins

THE CHRISTIAN MINDSET IN A SECULAR SOCIETY
© 1984 by Multnomah Press
Portland, Oregon 97266

Printed in the United States of America

Library of Congress Cataloging in Publication Data

Henry, Carl Ferdinand Howard, 1913–
    The Christian mindset in a secular society.
    Includes index.
    1. Sociology, Christian—Addresses, essays, lectures.
    2. Evangelicalism—Addresses, essays, lectures.
3. Civilization, Modern—1950–   —Addresses, essays,
lectures.   I. Title.
BT738.H42   1984   261.1   83-25136
ISBN 0-88070-041-6

86   87   88   89   90   91   –   10   9   8   7   6   5   4   3   2

Contents

Preface

I am pleased that Multnomah Press has collected these addresses on the assumption that they deserve hearing and reading beyond the audiences to which they were originally given. Some of the material has drawn secular press coverage, some has appeared in abridged form in one or another of the evangelical journals. But as a confrontation of the secular contemporary mood, the content appears in book format with distinct advantages. The Christian challenge to the prevalent secular spirit needs continually to be voiced on a broad front and in greater depth than a hurried media age often permits.

We need to hold the great biblical ideas and ideals before our shifting culture and to formulate these in words that will arrest the drift of modernity. Relativistic as our turning-time may be, we must not abandon it unprotested to unsound convictions. The trumpet call to truth and goodness has never been more imperative than in today's secular twilight, when the West seems incapable of making up its mind and when incisive critics tell us that our culture is crumbling, not so much because of alien powers but because of our own moral compromises and spiritual hesitancies.

If readers of this volume are aided in gaining perspective on the contemporary scene and spurred to proclaim and practice the vitalities of revealed religion, I shall be glad to have made, through the interest of the publisher, some modest additional contribution to meeting the need for helpful perspective on our times.

Trumpeting God's Word to a Nation in Decision

I am walking an evangelical tightrope—a raveling one, in fact. But I will nonetheless try to survive three maneuvers. First, I plead for a balanced verdict on our troubled nation; next, I assess some fearsome social trends; and finally, I project an evangelical counteroffensive.

A BALANCED VERDICT ON OUR TROUBLED NATION

Speaking for a national morality movement, an evangelical leader recently remarked: "The United States has turned away from God. It mocks God. It worships a twentieth century Baal . . . incarnated in sensuality, material goods, and immorality of every kind." Another spokesman described American society as "depraved, decadent and demoralized." Yet only a few years ago we were told that a new evangelical awakening had dawned in America; this very decade, it was said, is the decade of the evangelicals.

This address was first presented on 2 February 1983 at the fortieth annual convention of the National Religious Broadcasters held in Washington, D.C.

9

I reject both verdicts. Our vision is badly blurred if while we boast of forty million evangelicals we at the same time depict the United States as a nation of Baal worshipers. We need a sense of critical balance. Logically irreconcilable one liners may emulate Madison Avenue techniques, but they do little to serve either God's cause or our best evangelical interest.

While our country is great among the modern nations—great in resources, in power, in benevolence, and in performance—it nonetheless accommodates grave sin and great injustice. Sooner or later it will succumb to the essential finitude of earthly nations. It would be incalculably sad, however, if, having brought high blessing and hope to the modern world, the United States were to perish in young manhood, as it were, on the threshold of its greatest influence for global good.

The prime political issue of this century is liberty. Liberty under God to be sure, but liberty nonetheless. The prophets of freedom are dwindling. That is why we hear much more about peace than about liberty and the moral responsibility to deter predator powers. Man's lack of commitment to God means his inevitable spiritual enslavement to the world, while the loss of political freedom goes hand in glove with involuntary political bondage. Whenever totalitarian powers extend their frontiers they obscure Christ the liberator both spiritually and politically.

Yet military superiority in and of itself will not guarantee national permanence. Missiles provide no immunity from the divine dictum that "righteousness exalts a nation, but sin is a disgrace to any people" (Proverbs 14:34). As heralds of the gospel, we aim to bring this planet's skyways and sea-lanes and roadways into the service of the Creator of our cosmos and the Redeemer of our renegade race. Christ is heaven's last Word. In his judgment of men and nations, all the pseudolords will grope for words. The media will belatedly hail the Mediator; Christ the Great Communicator will be prime time.

How near God's final judgment may be—of the United States, of the Soviet Union, of China or Iran or Japan or of any other nation—I do not profess to know. No well-reasoned case exists for the unqualified superiority of Western culture over its rivals. I do not, however, consider the United States and the Soviet Union to be equally objectionable alternatives. Even less do I consider the Soviet Union and Marxism to be the bright channel of humanitarianism in our time. While some differences between the Free World and the Communist World are relative, the dissimilarities remain great indeed. I am convinced there is a Red gulag, but never have I heard of a red, white, and blue gulag. Those who mouth Marxist propaganda amid the privileged freedoms and comforts of the West know far less than Aleksandr Solzhenitsyn about the evils of communist rule. To say that material greed is what motivates capitalism while humanistic impulses are what motivate Marxism is more propaganda than truth. Marxist revolution has routinely worsened the social dilemmas it has sought to improve.

Religious freedom remains a great American distinctive. In principle, to be sure, it accommodates irreligion. The fact that human liberty is divorced increasingly from supernatural accountability may well become our national undoing. Yet a forced religious commitment is of no value either to God or to man. Freedom to worship and to serve the living God shelters all our other human liberties. We need not cope in America with an officially atheistic government dominated by political antichrists who approve for university teaching posts only cardholding communists intellectually hostile to the existence of a supernatural God. Free World agencies like the American Bible Society need not go underground to publish the Scriptures. The Bible is readily available throughout America in more translations than we need or read. American Protestants voluntarily give more than a billion dollars a year to missionary causes. Some fifty-five thousand of the eighty-five thousand Protestant missionaries serving overseas have been sent and supported by North American churches, the majority of these being evangelical congregations in the United States.

On balance the United States remains a force for good in the world, enviable and envied for many socioeconomic and cultural achievements. For good reason, distant refugees aspire to come to our shores, and multitudes closer to hand eagerly cross our borders for a larger stake in individual happiness.

"America right or wrong" is not an impassioned credo for me; a Christian can pledge unqualified allegiance only as long as any nation maintains itself "under God" and does not presume to be God. On the other hand I refuse to criticize the United States more than the U.S.S.R. or, like some of my friends, to criticize the U.S. more than Israel. To depict the United States mainly in terms of weaknesses and vices as politicians sometimes do in order to topple an incumbent from office, or as some evangelists and social critics may do to elicit decisions or funds, may hasten the eclipse of America as a model for authentic national possibility and spur interest in far less promising political alternatives. Maneuver number one: *We need to voice a balanced judgment on our troubled nation.*

AN ASSESSMENT OF FEARSOME SOCIAL TRENDS

Appalling social vices thrust us ever nearer a national doomsday. Only a pseudotheologian would ignore the emptiness that sweeps much of American life today and the deep social problems and injustices that scar our land. Many persons pursue but bursting bubbles of "vanity," as the writer of Ecclesiastes puts it. For multitudes human existence empties into meaninglessness.

Scholars spin grandiose theories of cosmic origins only to make less and less sense of human survival. In his book *The First Three Minutes: A Modern View of the Origin of the Universe,* the brilliant theoretical physicist Steven Weinberg remarks, "It is almost irresistible for humans to believe that we have some special relation to the universe, that human life is not just a more-or-less farcical outcome of a chain of accidents reaching back to the first three minutes, but that we were somehow built in from the beginning."[1] But then Weinberg hastens to tell us, in effect, that man stands in no such special relationship, that human life is but a purposeless outcome of accidental origins and that impersonal processes shape our existence. "It is very hard to realize that this . . . is . . . an overwhelmingly hostile universe. . . . It is even harder to realize that this present universe has evolved from an unspeakably unfamiliar early condition, and faces a future extinction of endless cold or intolerable heat. The more the universe seems comprehensible, the more it also seems pointless."[2]

Naturalism, in short, reduces the external world to mindless processes and events. It deprives personality of ultimately real status and thus jeopardizes the transcendent nature of all personal and social values. Is it any wonder life lived only in this drab gray context deprives human personality of meaning and worth?

This modern mood is not peculiarly American, of course, or unique to Western capitalist society. Disavowal of supernatural authority is a worldwide ingredient of the modern spirit. In totalitarian countries rulers artificially preserve authority by imposing freedom-eroding restraints upon the masses.

For at least a decade, however, secular humanism has stalked and penetrated the American university classroom. This masked metaphysics or covert conceptuality of contemporary liberal learning stifles the supernatural by suggesting that giving priority to God leads to indifference toward this world's misery. Meanwhile religious humanism has fed on leftovers of the very Christian theism that it rejects. But the agenda of social ethics advanced by humanism—including human dignity and human rights, ecological concerns and response to poverty—cannot long survive on the basis of a merely naturalistic theory of man and the world. On its naturalistic foundation, humanism is powerless to preserve human dignity and concern for human welfare. The universal moral imperatives of humanism cannot be logically supported by the premise that personality is an accidental by-product of an impersonal cosmic explosion, that all existence is time bound and transitory, that all ideas and ideals are the offshoot of the culture in which they appear, that man creatively imposes on history and nature whatever values they may have.

While American humanism inconsistently borrows the bare bones of a social ethic from the Judeo-Christian heritage, it ignores the great biblical mandate that man the creature is to love God the creator with his whole being. More than this, while it concentrates on social ideals, American humanism also muffles the divine call to holy personal living. The fact is that the remnants of conventional morality espoused by humanists are becoming less credible to a student generation indoctrinated in naturalistic prejudices. The consequent hodgepodge of illogical humanist dogma is unable therefore to stay the course and a more thoroughgoing naturalism takes over.

Today's pharisaism has forgotten what Jesus stressed: namely, that what is unclean is not external to man but lodges in his very heart and spirit. By contrast it views external social structures as alone wicked and mankind as their victim. The Bible teaches that no one—not the humanist, not the revolutionary, not even the most prestigious evangelical—is impervious to a contaminated self. One reason why many persons think sin is to be found mostly in society—notably in political institutions, social structures, and multinational corporations—is that they no longer sufficiently probe their own lives to admit where sin is really to be found. But we have all tasted the fruit of the forbidden tree; sin coils about us and lodges in our very being.

Now a new secular mindset is emerging, one that cares little about either unjust social structures or the sinful self. Seeking social escape from all the ethical demands of civilized existence, it considers almost everything irrelevant, just so long as one's actions express private decision and personal creativity. In other words, nothing matters but self-assertion. This is what some of our very neighbors and townspeople think even while we glory in the supposed heyday of the evangelical.

Let me say more. A marked deterioration in American society, indeed in Western society generally, has arisen at the very time when evangelicals have been emerging from the subculture into the culture. The implications of this fact are immensely important for Christian communication and apologetics generally and for every evangelical ministry specifically involved in mass media.

In earlier generations Americans judged themselves by Judeo-Christian principles even if they failed to live by them. But much of today's generation functions by a value system severed from the commandments of God and from supernatural accountability; it is oriented mostly to social utility. Many persons no longer know how to rejoice in life as an existence lived in communion with God, one filled by Spirit-given virtues and devoted under God to human service. The problem is far more than that the pressures of personal survival conspire with man's sinful bent to elevate self-interest above community-interest. What we are witnessing, rather, is human existence deliberately and routinely collapsed into a *me*-first philosophy—me first in sex, in work, in all dimensions of life.

This growing vanguard of society perceives what Christianity calls "the good life" to be a threat to self-fulfillment. For earlier generations the intimidating feature of Christian commitment was its rebuke to ungodliness and its reminder of future judgment. Today's narcissistic philosophy considers biblical imperatives a barrier to self-realization and the church an impediment to free and creative selfhood. Renewal of sinners in Christ's magnificent image is replaced by conceptions of a "new image" defined by physical gratification, material affluence, and worldly status.

The humanist mindset has been hostile to supernatural theism, revealed truths, and divine commandments for an entire generation. Now, besides disavowing the supernatural intellectually, the new vanguard also disowns all eternal authority existentially and deliberately orients life according to individual and personal disposition. Supernaturalism it disparages as myth—as an unbenevolent and retrogressive myth in fact—and thrusts aside Scripture's definition of the good life as unrewarding and undesirable, and as erosive of creative selfhood and personal fulfillment. Man is perceived as an animal oddity of nature, a mammalian masterpiece. His sex life is reduced to a series of stimulating encounters between biologically differing mates, events with no moral significance or religious answerability.

George Will writes of those who believe that "the good life is the glandular life." Chastity is considered prudery and unchastity a virtue. Not hell but herpes is what these moral rebels fear. We now must cope with a segment of society for whom abortion is good under any circumstances, for whom adultery and divorce are good, the nuclear family restrictive, incest therapeutic, and crime justified as social necessity.

While not every rebel against biblical morality, not every dropout from ethical humanism is devoted to this full calendar of evils, the defiance of inherited truth is nonetheless deliberate. The so-called new virtues of self-exaltation and ruthlessness replace traditional ones of self-humiliation and kindness. Self-denial and agape are scorned as weakness; self-indulgence and eros take their place.

The assumption is that one who is traditionally virtuous cannot be happy. The quest for personal pleasure must dictate all one's options and decisions. Self-fulfillment can embrace the swinging singles, homosexuality, lesbianism and prostitution, habitual divorce, routine remarriage, addiction to abortion, sexual abuse and exploitation of children. The litany of human savagery lengthens to include acts of terrorism aimed to achieve egoist objectives. When aides to a president who is avowedly a Christian believer say that he cannot attend church even at Christmas because of security problems it is time we are shocked awake.

Simply stated, American culture is at a fateful crossroads. The fortunes of all the West are now enmeshed with those of the Bible, as are the fortunes of this entire planet, in fact, to which the West carried the message of the self-revealing God. Indeed, much of Western civilization may already have made its decisive turn. Modern science, hailed a half century ago as the pinnacle of evolutionary progress and bright signal of the dawning kingdom of God, could by its proud nuclear capacities revert the earth in a single flash to a primeval wasteland. For all that, science is powerless to identify moral norms or final truth; scientific research asks what is experimentally possible, not what is morally permissible. Perhaps God will allow our wayward civilization to destroy itself by the very instruments and techniques whereon our generation relies for its distinctive greatness. Etched upon fallen history is a principle of justice that defies human perversity and does so through the very mechanisms that man puts forward to exalt himself.

The Bible will discredit any and all who use it to promote only self-serving ends. While Scripture validates the principles of private property, profit, and self-interest, it neither absolutizes these principles nor isolates them from other moral criteria. To be sure, the contrast between human rights and property rights is specious, for property rights are also human rights. Yet the fact remains that elevating economic interests to unqualified supremacy soon invites free enterprise's destruction from both within and without. Ideally self-interest and social-interest should coincide. But in man's present condition, self-interest tends toward self-gratification and requires constant correction. One need not gain the whole world to lose one's soul; succumbing to but an all-consuming part of it is quite enough. The Bible approves of self-love, but not at the cost of neighbor-love. It approves private property but only as others' property rights are respected. It approves profit but not exploitation. Above all the Bible calls us to responsible stewardship of both possessions and of profits. Today economic aspiration can all too often overshadow spiritual and ethical values. Madison Avenue victimizes both the merchant and the consumer. Baskin-Robbins, for example, promotes the gustatory delights of its chocolate sauce by using Handel's "Hallelujah Chorus" as background music. The publisher who eagerly prints *God's Bullies,* a critical appraisal of so-called morality mongers by an avowed homosexual, benefits from congenial reviews that lure gullible readers.

The media are inescapably implicated in shaping values. Much that they offer is commendable. I spent more than twenty years as a reporter and editor and have almost always been treated fairly by the press; I want likewise to be fair to the media. Among the great blessings of the Free World is freedom of the press. That tyrants and dictators try to suppress it is no surprise. Having said all this, we need nonetheless to guard against and to challenge the sordidness, the dramatized graffiti of a retrograde culture that airs periodically even on prime time television.

Some networks have at least begun to self-critically examine their prime time behavior. We should applaud such efforts and whatever improvements all three major networks have made in the recent past. Portrayal of violence and of gratuitous sex is still high, however. Television has sadly abolished the uniqueness of childhood; it promotes child abuse by thrusting on all youngsters regardless of age all manner of adult beliefs and role models. Recently an eleven-year-old—enrolled in Christian day school at that—asked his teacher: "How does one say 'let's go to bed' in French?" We need, moreover, to monitor the propaganda role of television writers, producers, and sponsors, lest they turn church-state separation into an artifice simply to prevent moral pressure on the networks. One recent telecast of nudist scenes taken at a sex therapy group party carried "King of Kings and Lord of Lords" as background music. Let it be known loud and clear: If we must choose between the American television industry and Christ, between writers, producers, or sponsors and Christ, we will unequivocally opt for Jesus Christ.

But do we evangelicals as well perhaps sell Christ short and cheaply? In preserving a Christian home that prepares children to take their place in society as persons of godly faith and service, we perhaps face our most important missionary opportunity. Training children in the Way is a matter of parental duty. The rebellious child in your own home who on occasion is tempted to tell you to go to the eschatological unmentionable may be the most important potential leader you will ever direct into the service of Christ.

Are we not in part responsible for the perversion of media liberty? How effectively do we, in life and literature, exhibit the supremacy of agape over eros? Why, for example, despite the many evangelical film enterprises in America, was it a secular British company that produced award-winning *Chariots of Fire*, a spectacle whose success evangelical agencies exploited by belatedly portraying the hero's larger missionary role?

Must we not implore almighty God for new vision? Traditional evangelical hand-me-downs are inadequate for this turning-time in history. Easily vocalized pieties and hurried sermonic clichés may continue to attract those whose dream bubbles have popped and who welcome some convenient escape hatch while they try to flee this planet. However, for those for whom cosmic nature is the sum total of reality, for whom impersonal processes define the source and context of human existence, and for whom moral distinctions simply illustrate private preferences, many present preaching routines resemble an attempt to revive a person whose heart will not respond.

What distinguishes the present moral decline in America from that of earlier generations? Simply this: Today's secular *mind*set rests as never before upon a nonbiblical *will*set.

Of course when I speak of a human *will*set against the revealed will of God, you know enough theology to reply that fallen man's will has throughout history been steeled by nature against the will of the Creator. The Bible declares man as sinner to be not a lover of God but a hater of God. We know also that despite contemporary man's *will*set against his Maker, God's image, however sullied, remains even now a point of contact for divine confrontation. Yet, as Paul reminds the Romans, pagan rebellion in ancient times actually escalated until God irrevocably "gave them over" (Romans 1:24, 26, 28). That is, the Creator responded to mankind's insistent and unyielding rejection of him by finally abandoning rebellious humanity to its own determinate intellectual depravity, degrading passions, and moral impurity. Now the West is reverting to its pagan and pre-Christian readiness to murder the innocents and the defenseless, to destroy unwanted infants, to dispose of the maimed and elderly, and even to massacre neighboring enemy populations. The fact is that an alarming number of our contemporaries, people within easy reach of the gospel of Christ, are moving irrevocably beyond simply a rebellious conscience to a corrupt conscience, one which not only stifles the truth of God and suppresses the awareness of future judgment, but actually delights in sin and commends those who practice it.

The special distinctive of a democracy, some sociologists now tell us, is its tolerance of divergent views. Tolerance thus becomes a rationale for uncritical public acceptance of any and all deviation. But the founding American fathers never declared or even intended that tolerance be an excuse or basis for dissolving all norms. Standing by itself, tolerance destroys even itself in destroying all norms. The perverse notion that democracy is incompatible with moral absolutes spells for democracy inevitable collapse into chaos. The flipside implication of this notion is that only totalitarian powers deal in moral absolutes, a conclusion that credits tyrants with being monitors of the good. The fact is, of course, that by arbitrarily imposing universal rules tyrants simply reduce the good to bureaucratic preference.

Only the most stupid of souls will fail to see how bleak is America's prospect if she opts ongoingly for sensual gratification and crass self-fulfillment. As John Wesley put it, "a studied inattention to the invisible, eternal world, an indifference to death and its consequences" leads to the tragic unhallowing of human life. Tightrope maneuver two: *The rampant moral iniquity of our era brings us perilously near a civilizational endtime.* Our nation continues to be spared from ruin—believe it!—not by technological genius, not by political wisdom, not by economic expertise, but by the forbearing mercy of God despite those who no longer "glorified him as God nor gave thanks to him" (Romans 1:21).

AN EVANGELICAL COUNTEROFFENSIVE

Can we turn the tide? Have we the resources to transpose secular society's current plight into a program of spiritual aspiration and moral earnestness? Albert Outler speaks of "Christian alternatives to the now finally discredited experiments in autonomy." Is that mere millennial enthusiasm?

For all our impressive numbers, for all our larger public visibility, for all our varied ministries with multimillion-dollar budgets, Kenneth Kantzer, advisory editor of *Christianity Today,* says candidly that evangelical Christianity is now weaker in America than it was fifteen years ago. In the early years when evangelicals numbered only one in ten, their national influence was "infinitely greater than the evangelical influence today."[3] In a culture where forty to fifty million persons claim to be born again and where evangelists emphasize their growing harvest of conversions, the statistics of abortion, divorce, alcoholism and drug addiction, rape and murder nonetheless continue to mount. A disconcertingly wide segment of American society succumbs to the premise that life has not come from God, does not move toward God, and cannot be enriched by God.

One disturbing possibility, of course, is that evangelical agencies with ready funding may have too little depth and vision to cope with the current conflict. God's kingdom is built not on per-

petual motion, one liners, and flashbulbs but on Christ, his sure
Word. What counts is not how many enterprises we create, but
why we create them and how worthily and effectively we maintain
them. I come therefore to maneuver three: *We need to get on with
more effective evangelical engagement in the public arena.*

Evangelical preaching clouds an understanding of "the good
life" if it accommodates the self-fulfillment trend by failing to distinguish the old self that needs crucifixion from the new self or new
character that the Holy Spirit nurtures. Decision for Christ makes
us whole (we are now sometimes told) with a wholeness that embraces not only spiritual and moral well-being, but pledges physical and financial well-being also. Compound this with sexual
fulfillment and—total bliss!—one caters completely to the worldly
agenda of self-satisfaction. The rub is that the world itself suspects
that genuine spiritual commitment and moral restraint render ques-
tionable an infinity of material affluence and sex, and that Christian
wholeness is something quite different from what secular society
espouses. The current philosophy "be born again and God will put
you in clover" needs divine editing to read "get right with God and
he will show you how many excesses you can do without."

One sure way to frustrate evangelical awakening is for Christians to effusively give Sunday to God but, for the rest of the week,
to accommodate a secular lifestyle shaped by craven greed. Let us
show the world what life made whole truly is. Our secular contemporaries often equate great living with great self-indulgence rather
than with self-giving; to them, nothing seems more dubious than
the emphasis that the way to find one's life is to lose it. But if we are
ambiguous about modeling the evangelical lifestyle, if we have no
heart to die to self, no longing for Christ's return because that
would end our privileged comforts, then what right have we to
judge the world? The incongruity between how we ought to live
and how much we ape our contemporaries needs to disturb us. We
need to chafe under the Savior's example—the lives he touched,
the way he spent his days, the security he found in God. His
portfolio carried no heavenly investment in the perpetuity of the
Roman Empire or even in the real estate of Palestine.

I hold no brief for Marxist theory, of course, which has

nowhere made good on its promise of economic utopia—and never will. Free enterprise has immense values over against the bureaucratically controlled societies. I do not find in the Old Testament a single prophet or in the New Testament a single apostle who considers private property an evil; nor do I find the Christ of the Gospels equalizing the wealth either of the Jews or of the Romans of his day as the path to social or spiritual utopia. Stripped of moral answerability, however, free enterprise soon invites ethical censure by sensitive social critics and by ideologists given to socialist alternatives. More importantly, when free enterprise frees itself of God it invites the judgment of God. As we know, communism and socialism impede rather than help the Christian cause; while Christianity does not depend upon capitalist economics, a truly viable capitalism does depend upon moral principle. Marxism is a cruel economic hoax that inflames the material aspirations of the masses and exploits their discontents. But secular capitalism as an ethically unbridled economic philosophy likewise arouses the desire for material excess and indulgence. It may not please some evangelical empire builders to be reminded that an unqualified endorsement of current economic philosophy may abet the spread of secularism. On the other hand some business executives are more aware and troubled than are their own pastors by the greed that engulfs the American perspective, even that of Christians. Let us not uncritically commend what we better than others should know is constantly vulnerable to corruption.

Without strong commitments to justice, our call to Christ and to evangelical awakening will be feeble. Growing evangelical concern not only with biblical preaching and personal evangelism but also with social imperatives is a big plus. Some who speak for evangelical social justice today lose credibility because they voice unfortunate clichés. Social and political invective will never solve the problems of this spiritually askew planet, nor will increased evangelical conversions automatically do so, let alone government deficit spending. Yet our participation must offer authentic hope to people who are hurting. We need an evangelical coalition, one neither dominated nor exploited by existing agencies, to forge a broad consensus over against the major social evils of our time.

The Bible espouses the dignity and desirability of work. We cannot minimize the demeaning impact of joblessness upon workers to whom God entrusted worthy vocational gifts. In a healthy society joblessness is as great a concern as the plight of the needy. But a society that responds voluntarily to its needs is superior to one in which the welfare of humanity becomes the sole responsibility of government. The plight of Polish workers is a grim reminder that bureaucratic supervision of human welfare can be far from benevolent.

I commend caring churches that are alert to the work needs of their members and that maintain a pantry and clothes closet open to needy townspeople. I commend Christian agencies like World Vision that have reached out compassionately wherever staggering human need stares at us. May their standing example stimulate Hindus and Muslims to respond similarly to famished hordes in India, Bangladesh, Pakistan, and Indonesia.

Consider what the initiative and example of the dedicated individual can achieve. No longer are we limited to role models of eighteenth century Britain. During and after the Korean War, Bob Pierce launched an orphan ministry that spawned World Vision's program of international compassion and concern. Chuck Colson emerged from post-Watergate repentance to confront the conscience of evangelicals, first in America and then around the world, with the needs of millions of spiritually and judicially neglected prisoners.

Vital as they are, however, social concerns must not obscure the need of personal conversion and the importance of holy living. When we think of Jesus Christ, his holiness is what immediately comes to mind. It is tragic indeed that not even evangelical leaders now escape the ethical lassitude or even the moral failure of the secular world. Is the world then overpowering the church that ought to be penetrating the world? Does not the New Testament warn us that not only the world but even the professing church may shelter the demonic? Was not Judas one of the Twelve? Church renewal requires not only the majestic truth of the Bible but also the dynamic work of the Holy Spirit. The laity are waiting for the clergy (and God may be waiting for them as well) to lead the way to his holy presence and to a bold thrust for our cities and for our nation.

Yet how sad it is that in a single generation experiential and existential concerns have come so largely to overshadow interest in theology that the great doctrines of the faith survive only like a few shredded nuts loosely scattered over ice cream. In my Christian college days the rugged discipline of philosophy was the most popular major on campus; no senior was graduated without a course in logic and without mastering James Orr's *Christian View of God and the World*. In graduate studies we confidently set evangelical theism alongside rival worldviews in pursuit of the whole truth. Some of us eagerly left the security of well-established jobs to plant a new seminary on the then evangelically neglected West coast. A handful of us launched *Christianity Today* in 1956 to give the *Christian Century* a run for its prejudices. Not even a lonely fifteen-year project like *God, Revelation and Authority* seemed too great a burden to carry in trying to reach the human mind, the human conscience, the human will for God and his Christ.

Kenneth Kantzer attributes today's weakened evangelical influence not simply to cultural changes but also to the fact that our constituency includes too few of the intellectual elite. We are in desperate need of a renewal of evangelical intellectual life. Never has the need for media presentation of the Christian worldview been more urgent. Why should sunrise semester television be preempted by only humanists? Could not our network of sturdy evangelical colleges, some boasting communications centers, use the media to present the case for God and biblical theism? In earlier generations great colleges were deliberately established to reflect the intellectual credentials of Christianity. When that heritage was obscured or neglected, these schools soon became seedbeds of Enlightenment modernism and then of religious humanism. Is today's evangelical community so bereft of academic and financial resources that it can make no credible case for supernatural transcendence in the media age? And can we not rally a first-rate panel of evangelical minds to address moral and spiritual dilemmas and to speak to the conscience of the nation?

Successful evangelical business leaders sponsor all manner of media activity with no focus on the issues that now decide the fate of civilization in our time. What this nation needs is not more personal or organizational promotional hype, not proclamation of how great you and I are or think we are (or that our public relations departments are salaried to say we are), but rather a presentation of the great and all-encompassing truth and grace of God that alone can make us wise and good and happy. Whether people want to hear it or not, we are mandated to declare the truth of revelation competently and, moreover, to declare it winsomely, so that some who may not want to hear it may hear it nonetheless. So it was when you and I came to Christ. And so, if God be pleased, it can and will be for our contemporaries and for this now dying civilization to which the Holy Spirit even today extends the possibility of new life in Christ.

"Trumpeting God's Word to a Nation in Decision," Notes

1. Steven Weinberg, *The First Three Minutes: A Modern View of the Origin of the Universe* (New York: Basic Books, 1977), p. 154.

2. Weinberg, *First Three Minutes*, p. 154.

3. "Reflections: Five Years of Change," *Christianity Today*, 26 November 1982, p. 15.

Theology for Our Day

A s a university student trembling on the brink of exams for the doctorate in philosophy, I joined with others in a hunt for clues to the kind of questions we might face. We entreated graduate assistants and young professors for such clues, but they stonewalled us. Finally, on the morning of exams, one of them volunteered a word of advice. "All the questions," he said, "are like this: Explain the universe and give two or three examples."

The fact is, theology fits this challenge remarkably well: it is a picture window on God, on the universe he has created, and on the world to come.

At the heart of the word theology is *theos,* the living God. Its study awakens mighty motifs like Bible, Creation and Church, Humanity and History, Redemption and Resurrection, State and Society, at whose center is the living God of Grace and Glory.

Yet beyond even these great themes theology speaks to me first and foremost of silence—silence in heaven, silence on earth, silence that only God can shatter. Above that silence we hear his

This address was first presented in May 1981 in several major Canadian cities at meetings sponsored by clergy and lay leaders of the Evangelical Fellowship of Canada.

voice: "And God said, 'Let there be' . . . and there was . . ." (Genesis 1:3ff.). "Hear the word of the LORD, O nations; proclaim it in distant coastlands" (Jeremiah 31:10).

We would profit from the silencing of today's media barrage. Our tongue-polluted culture thrusts upon us endless soap operas and talk shows we could do without, a parade of automobiles, perfumes, and record albums that we neither want nor need, and novel philosophies and moral aberrations that we ought to avoid and flee. Madison Avenue prospers on a genius for disguising the truth and distorting the word.

As Christians we need to tune our spirits to God's heavenly Talk-Show: to the God who *speaks* his own word, the God who *shows* himself throughout the cosmos and history, and who supremely *shows himself* in Jesus Christ. This Divine Speaker is waiting for people to converse with him, to spend unhurried time with him, the God of the Ages, the Eternal One who wants more than a three-minute long distance call or a five-minute parking stop for a 'hello' and 'goodbye.' Activism today so hurries evangelical worship, prayer, and Bible reading, theological study and reflection, that we risk becoming practical atheists steeped in this-worldly priorities. Theological renewal is a farce apart from time for God in his Word. Is it too much to ask Christians in favored North America, in their struggle to be evangelically authentic, to do their theological homework once again, to feast on mighty truths that can rebuff the blows of an ungodly age, to learn biblical lessons before the sword and dungeons overtake them? "Be still," says Yahweh. "Be still, and know that I am God" (Psalm 46:10).

THE GOSPEL OF JESUS CHRIST

Counterfeit theologies inundate our earth. Theologians of the absurd espouse paradox. Skyrocket theologians promote existentialism. Nonsense theologians defer to logical positivism. Mixmaster theologians entangle the Creator in space-time. Cataclysm theologians trust violence to turn the world right side up. One after another, creative modern theologians zoom their spaceships above the stratosphere only to precipitate a series of devastating splashdowns from outer space because each retains far too few biblical components.

Will the real theologians please stand up? ask the confused masses. They ask it in Japan, where 60 percent of the population espouses no religion. They ask it in England where 750,000 resident Muslims and 250,000 Hindus are refurbishing some of the redundant urban churches into temples. While King Khalid of Saudi Arabia exhorts thirty-seven Muslim rulers to Muslim law and Islamic fundamentals, visiting Muslim theologians in London remind followers that among leading British churchmen some debunk the New Testament as *The Myth of God Incarnate*. Moonies and Hare Krishnas have invaded the West. Along with the masses of refugees from Southeast Asia has come a new wave of oriental religions, even while America reels with horrendous memories of Jonestown and copes with spreading Scientology and multiplying Mormonism. Visitation committees complain that a Mormon has gotten there before them and that Jehovah's Witnesses are often close behind. Meanwhile ecumenical churches debate how theological pluralism best copes with the diversity of the cults. As the end of the second millennium looms amid the deepening pressures for human survival, speculation mounts about the End of all ends and prophecy-mongers review new candidates for the Antichrist.

But does this modern proliferation of nonbiblical faiths differ greatly, after all, from the many mystery religions, strange philosophies, and exotic cults that haunted the ancient world of Christian beginnings? Did not Jesus himself warn: "I have come in my Father's name, and you do not accept me; but if someone else comes in his own name, you will accept him"? (John 5:43). And did not Paul the apostle, in a world not essentially unlike our own, address to both Jew and Gentile the message of God's present anger against man's wickedness and of God's proffer of redemptive rescue?

Had the living God spoken but a single sentence, had man's Creator uttered but one intelligible imperative, ought not every one of us to "stop, look, and listen"? In "A Mighty Fortress is our God," Luther menaces the Prince of darkness: "One little word shall fell him. That word, above all earthly powers, No thanks to them—abideth!"

Consider with me some living and abiding words, words of the Word become flesh, of the eternal Christ who is Christianity's cornerstone, and let us propel them into our present day. "I am come," Christ declares (Matthew 5:17, KJV), and thus calls all mankind to personal decision about the promised Messiah who was to step into fallen history. "I am *come,*" he says; "*I am* come"; "*I* am come." Christianity centers in Christ's person and work, his incarnation, death, and resurrection. Christianity is, of course, more than Christ. But without Christ there can be no Christian and no Christianity. One is left simply with the itty-bitty: promise without fulfillment, sacrifice without atonement, death without resurrection, godhead without triunity. "I am come!" If Christ is excised or moved to the margin, theology fails both Christianity and our contemporary world. The eternal Christ alone supplies history's midpoint and will return to define its endpoint. All who search for a Constant in this age of relativities—relative to power, to time, to culture—can be assured, can know that *I am* has come and that he who has come endures: "Jesus Christ is the same yesterday and today and forever" (Hebrews 13:8).

We need therefore to declare once again the biblical basics of divine promise and fulfillment; namely, that Messiah would come and disclose himself in the midst of humanity, that the Spirit would come to individually indwell God's people, that God's redeemed *ecclesia* would embrace Gentiles as well as Jews to acknowledge his saving power to the ends of the earth, and that Christ crucified and risen from the dead will return to judge the nations of mankind.

Instead of allowing Western worship of the Golden Calf to wizen our souls, we must allow the penetrating truth of biblical theology to reshape our spiritual and moral universe. Only faithfulness to the *I am* who is light and life, bread from heaven and living water, the resurrection and the life, will nurture Christian stalwarts like Aleksandr Solzhenitsyn and Georgi Vins whom communist imprisonment could not silence, martyrs like Chester Bitterman the murdered Wycliffe translator, and other stouthearted saints like those on whom Nero's lions feasted. "Take up [your] cross and follow me," said Jesus (Mark 8:34). Do any nails scar us deeply enough to suggest a costly agony? "I am come," says Jesus. May nothing hold a higher place on our agenda than Jesus Christ. The world today looks and waits for another; evangelical, make known the *I am* who has already come!

THE CHURCH

Perhaps Christ's word about the church is one that evangelicals just now need most to hear. In our day evangelicals must not be content to display the defects of the ecumenical establishment. Those flaws are apparent enough. In the last seventeen years nine denominations in the National Council of Churches have lost 5 million members. Of these 1.1 million were among Methodists alone, despite their annual national and regional budgets of $200 million and their thirty thousand local churches. Among the United Presbyterians, fifty-three congregations, including some of the best known, have withdrawn from that denomination during the past five years. The Roman Catholic Church has grown only because of Hispanic immigration. Mainline Protestant denominations are under fire for funding revolutionary movements, compromising confessional theology, and yielding to parachurch groups the initiative for evangelical causes like student evangelism, scripture translation, orphan and child care, and pro-life concerns.

Many evangelical churches meanwhile have shown marked growth. Their members are biblically literate; they support evangelism and overseas missionary causes; they are devoted to humanitarian programs of world relief, development assistance, and prison reform; and their members have become increasingly active in political concerns.

There is something disconcerting, however, about the growing stress on local superchurches and superpastors that often neglects the larger organic unity of the whole family of believers. Do evangelicals really care what Jesus Christ says about the church? Does what he declares about ecclesiology matter as much to us as what he says about evangelism? Can a church divided and subdivided and subsubdivided truly be Christ's church? Does merely rejecting or absolving oneself of an ecumenical institutional badge justify the lack of evangelical interrelationships and of coordinated fellowship? Does not a society succumbing to secularism demand a comprehensive local and national witness? More importantly, does not the biblical ideal of the church demand more of us?

Why do some clergymen, disenchanted with pluralistic ecumenism, (and also some conservative evangelical young people), seriously consider a return to Rome? Is it only because they prefer, as some do, a dimension of ritual in worship—which for that matter some Protestant churches also offer? Is it because recent papal encyclicals—infallible or not—often seem more carefully nuanced than the hasty pronouncements of Protestant ecumenists or the nonpronouncements of Protestant evangelicals?

The reason in more instances than we admit is that evangelicals do not seem to take seriously the singular unity of Christ's church. We privately feel that a united evangelical orthodoxy would not only move mountains but could perhaps even rescue and realign a morally and spiritually mired planet. But how do we translate this conviction into reality? We tend to resign ourselves uncritically to, and even to enthusiastically accept, our existing divisions. We limit cooperative effort to an annual convention or to triennial or quadrennial evangelistic campaigns. Massive parachurch groups, some not even in existence at midcentury, now further complicate the chaos of evangelical plurality.

Every appeal to an inerrant Bible should humiliate us before the inerrant Christ's insistence on the unity of his church. When at Caesarea Philippi Peter affirms Jesus to be the Christ, Jesus says: "On this rock I will build my *church*" (Matthew 16:18)—not many but one. As Sheldon Vanauken remarks, Christ spoke of his church "in the singular" and not in "the 10,000 sect plural."[1] When Jesus prays for the Holy Father to keep his disciples "one as we are one" (John 17:11), he forecloses our easy escape to fragmentation. Does the unity current among evangelicals truly reflect the unity of the Godhead?

I am in no way suggesting that organizational conglomerates or institutional megadenominations fulfill Christ's requirement.

But have we made credible the present reality of a deeply united ecclesial entity? Do we in principle oppose the endless proliferation of splinter groups? Is it any gain for biblical ecclesiology if we reject pluralistic ecumenism but at the same time approve pluralistic evangelicalism? In Washington, D.C., for example, three thousand active ministries that spend over $1 billion annually have little to do with each other. Can the evangelical enterprise long thrive at a national level—let alone world level—if it disregards and shrugs off what divides Christ's church at the local level? Does the sense of evangelical family, of one organism or body, extend beyond our particular assembly? We must break out of our evangelical subcultures and ecclesial rivalries to address our age as something more than a mobile movement trying to stay just a step ahead of a runaway society.

But does the sense of evangelical family and the treasure of Christian fellowship always prevail even at the local level? Millions of Protestants, many evangelicals among them, choose and change their churches as they do their airlines—for convenience of travel, comfort, and economy. Multitudes have made crusade decisions but have not become members of a local congregation. Must we not address with new resolve the question of the character of the one regenerate family that constitutes Christ's church? Can we transcend the perception of evangelical chaos and rivalry by laying hold of something more identifiable as brotherly love?

If we seriously hope to shape these times, we cannot remain in a state of suspended animation between ecumenical pluralism for which enthusiasm has died, and evangelical unanimity that accommodates observable disunity. We must encourage theological fidelity, evangelistic earnestness, and community concern, without at the same time neglecting what Jesus meant by his *church,* his unique church that reflects the unity embodied by the Father and the Son and, let us add, the Spirit. The early church was known for its steadfast devotion "to the apostles' teaching and to the fellowship, to the breaking of bread and to prayer" (Acts 2:42). Does our present reality fully mirror this Pentecostal model? Would the apostles give us a passing grade? Will we allow Christ's own word to interrogate us? Will we let the Holy Spirit melt our irresolution? We must make ecclesiology a chief item of theological concern in order to more fully manifest what it means to be Christ's one church.

The communist projection of a proletarian world brotherhood has turned hollow. The political version of a universal brotherhood based on human equality has ground to a halt. Christ lives and waits to lift above the nadir of nothingness every human trapped in the debris of our collapsing civilization. Let us take to heart Jesus' word: *my church!* Like a beacon light sweeping the heavens, the evangelical church must beckon lost multitudes to the sure port of Christ's redeeming grace, to the new society already in the making whose creator and perfector is God.

THE BIBLE

Another mighty word for this decade is Jesus' pronouncement, "the Scripture cannot be broken" (John 10:35).

The fate of the Bible is the fate of Christianity and even of civilization itself. If the world neglects or evangelicals forsake this Book, the end result is society's inevitable theological, spiritual, and moral suicide. Neither social activism nor evangelical world congresses nor charismatic experiences will gain much in the long run unless the Bible is on their side. No text in the history of thought has so transformed human life as has this inspired book. The Epistle to the Romans alone held Augustine captive after he heard the voice, *Tolle, lege* (take up and read). For Martin Luther the book's good news of justification by faith shattered his torturous struggle for salvation by works. Karl Barth, by its declaration of special revelation and redemption, was turned against the high tide of Protestant modernism. Apart from the Bible no firm reply exists against the rampant unbelief and strident skepticism of our age, no sure way around the contorted detours of modern culture, no lasting alternative to the extraordinary evils that plague our generation.

We need to sound this authoritative biblical message and to rest on its divine inspiration. Jesus engaged in the controversy over its inerrancy by telling the Sadducees who clouded concerns of social ethics and eschatology: "You are in error because you do not know the Scriptures or the power of God" (Matthew 22:29).

The fact is, however, that the focus of the Bible debate has already shifted beyond inerrancy to interpretation and to revelation-and-culture concerns. For some scholars, Scripture functions authoritatively not by conveying fixed doctrinal truths but only by changing believers internally. We are indeed to be "doers" and not simply "hearers" of the Word (James 1:22). Our profit-oriented society flinches at Jesus' disconcerting question: "What good is it for a man to gain the whole world, yet forfeit his soul?" (Mark 8:36). But even these truths we know simply because Scripture is a corpus of revealed information about God and his purposes and deeds; it is profitable, among other things, for doctrine. For others the Bible represents but the thought-forms of ancient cultures. But Bruce Nichols properly insists, in his *Contextualization: A Theology of Gospel and Culture,* on the nonnegotiability of all the revealed transcultural truths about God himself, his creative and redemptive work, his cosmic and historical purposes, his mighty commands and great commission.

While those who reject the Bible and who think that modern learning has destroyed the miraculous may sometimes cling to theologically tolerant churches, they must be plainly told that they are not Christians. After two thousand years of scriptural consensus it is too late, as Harry Blamires reminds us, to redefine Christianity.[2]

Yet we are too much preoccupied with the Bible's existential impact and the private encouragement it affords us in times of personal crisis. To be sure, the preached word must intersect human life at its most critical moments—must speak to individuals engulfed by ethical vacuums, torn by consuming grief, battered by doubts, badgered by guilt, and hurting all over. But churchgoers too often treat the Bible like a jigsaw puzzle, arranging and rearranging random cutouts into an enigmatic chaos. Expository preaching should strive for congregational study of the text not only after but in preparation for church services. Thus prepared, God's gathered people will anticipate and experience corporate renewal by the Spirit and the Word in worship and response.

Instead of channeling the biblical text only into internal congregational response, important as that is, we must relate it also to nature and history and to human conscience universally. We need an expository ministry that brings forward into the civilizational crisis of the present the lessons of God's actions in the biblical past, and that stresses God's truth and power for our age. We must not blur the emphasis on God's external providence in history and the cosmos, nor fail to stress that naturalistic science, philosophy, and ethics rest on false assumptions about the real world. In the very cosmos that modern scientists investigate and in the very history that contemporary historians evaluate, the living God manifests himself and works out his sovereign purposes. While secular methodologies may arbitrarily exclude him, God remains nonetheless the God of nature and history.

The preached Word must speak to society in general, to great modern cities whose clichés about urban renewal fade into discouragement. Beset by crime and vice, callous to death, trapped in poverty, aching with joblessness, besieged by inflation and taxation, they look to lotteries more than to the Living Word. Who any longer dares to suggest that the Big Apple may be rotten at the core, that monstrous demons may inhabit the City of the Angels, that the Windy City may as justly be targeted by the last Whirlwind as was ancient Rome, that proud centers like Vancouver, Toronto, and Montreal may meet the fate of Nagasaki and Hiroshima? Almost no one today speaks of these metropolises as Jesus spoke of Tyre and Sidon; almost no one weeps over them as Jesus wept over Jerusalem; almost no one seems aware that they may be but hurried whistle stops on God's judgment trail. Who today trumpets the theme that God is sovereign in the city, that the great universities and fearless media are answerable to him? Who declares that the Judge of all the earth requires just judges, impartial law enforcement officers, fair news reporters and editors?

Biblical truth—transcultural as it is—has an indispensable message for contemporary culture. It addresses modern learning, modern ethics, modern politico-economic concerns, and all the idolatries of our polytheistic society. It proclaims the gospel to a generation that is intellectually uncapped, morally unzipped, and volitionally uncurbed. Those who consider the latest fads permanently "in" will, of course, dismiss the Christian message as the last hurrah of an antiquated outlook. They reveal their sickness of soul by derogating terms like morality, piety, family, work, patriotism, born again, evangelical, theology. Christianity they dismiss as a kind of middle-class hedonism. Declaring it intellectually inadmissible, they meanwhile espouse a life that neither reason nor conscience nor spirit can support or condone. Repression of sensuality and of self-gratification they call psychotically abnormal; subordination of the flesh they leave to medieval monks or consign to the future resurrection. Affirming sexual pleasure to be the supreme good of a life of unending revelry, they waste away into ethical ghosts and skeletons.

In the United States, 2.5 million unmarried adults are living together. Over 11.5 million one-parent homes dot our land, many of them due not to death but to divorce and teenage pregnancies. In an age when 150 million women use contraceptive pills whose physical consequences carry indeterminate risk, the technical definition of "family" now covers parents having no marriage contracts. To our shame Russia, whose totalitarian and atheistic motivations repel our democratic instincts, promotes traditional family values and home stability more effectively than does American society.

Biblical ethics boldly and clearly addresses the abyss of immorality engulfing our technological civilization; it speaks to greed for money, to lust for sexual pleasure, to crime, murder, terrorism, arson, and other hallmarks of our warped society. It confronts all of modern life—its perverted sense of the good, its banalities and superficialities, its mythology of technocratic utopianism, its triumphal evils. In a world whose nuclear arms can already pulverize civilization overnight and which fears the horrendous unforeseen consequences of nuclear waste and pollution, the Soviet Union in 1980 alone spent $175 billion and the United States $115 billion for defense.

Our evangelistic courage dare not be broken by the immensity of these problems. Because we have an inviolable Word of God to proclaim, we must constantly reinforce not only the ineradicable sense of God that remains but also whatever basic sensitivities and impulses to ethical decency survive. The gospel must remain central, for it alone can beam radiance into the lives of those who, having traded purity for pleasure, now turn from pleasure to psychiatry to salvage their souls. Once discussed only privately within the family, intimacies of life are now public domain except for one particular theme—death.

Scripture throughout openly declares and illumines the reality of death—physical, moral, or spiritual. The world, on the other hand, clothes death only in euphemism: people, we are told, are "laid to rest" or "pass away." Can evangelical deathstyle perhaps witness to this generation about God as much as evangelical lifestyle? Death and life are forefront biblical themes and nowhere more conspicuously so than in the good news, the evangel. This is of supreme importance, Paul writes, "that Christ died for our sins according to the Scriptures, that he was buried, that he was raised on the third day according to the Scriptures, and that he appeared . . ." (1 Corinthians 15:3-5). As portrayed in the Bible, death is a transition from life to life; that is, from creation life to resurrection life. The quality of that life, moreover, depends on whether or not we participate in redemption life.

Scripture cannot be broken, says Jesus: the apostolic message is what the Bible teaches. We need a generation devoted to biblical priorities, not to personal predelictions. We need to banner the apostolic kerygma, not the trendy come-ons of our age. The latest trends will all be shattered, but Scripture has timeless durability.

MISSION

Climaxing these theological proposals for our day are two more words by Jesus. Although we usually associate them, each of the words is important in its own right. So far we have mentioned christology, the incarnational center of the doctrine of God: "I am come"; then ecclesiology, Jesus' concern for his singular church; and bibliology, the comprehensive rule of faith and practice. Now we come to missiology.

Some will think at once, and appropriately enough, of the Great Commission. A church without evangelism invites extinction; it raises doubts, moreover, about its spiritual vitality. According to the Thailand Consultation on World Evangelization, the church needs two hundred thousand missionaries if all peoples are to be reached by the year 2000. Recruiting, replacing, and effectively supporting missionary forces is of prime urgency. (When next you indulge, remember that coffee in Argentina is $2 a cup; a modest car sells for $28,000.) Not only new overseas but also new home ministries are needed. For the latter, naturalized Asians and Christian international students represent good prospects for witnessing effectively among Indochinese refugees with a heritage of oriental religions.

Too often, however, the church's mission has been limited to preoccupation with personal evangelism at the expense of public concerns, a disjunction that has provoked conflict over Christian involvement in the political arena. In the parable of the nobleman, the servants are instructed to carry forward the master's business, to be about the master's affairs during his absence in the far country. The King James translation, *"Occupy* till I come" (Luke 19:13), accommodates the conception of an army of occupation that challenges the power of Satan, who is really a squatter. We think too little of the cosmos and of human history as arenas where we as God's people are to resist satanic forces and to advance God's truth and justice. Jesus spoke of the illuminating and preserving role of Christians as light and salt in a darkening and decaying society.

This decade may erupt into a time of supercrises—a time of trouble beyond present comprehension when inflation and unemployment worsen the heartbreak plight of the destitute; a time of crippling energy depletion, ecological pollution, dread military aggression and political enslavement, moral and spiritual decline beyond imagination. Could the very last days engulf us when, as Paul says, many will "maintain a facade of 'religion'" while obscuring its power (2 Timothy 3:5, Phillips), and who, as Peter writes, "promise . . . freedom, while they themselves are slaves of depravity"? (2 Peter 2:19).

We must address the world's skepticism over moral norms, its distaste for work, the soaring crime rate, the need of prison reform, mushrooming pornography and weak obscenity laws. The statistics of the masses of persons who attend porno films weekly and of the "top ten" men's magazines that gross a half million dollars annually curdle the soul. Television has helped inure us to the lustful look and casual sex, to prostitution and adultery, while it devalues evangelical morality as a vestigial remnant of the dinosaur age. Advertising sells its wares by titillating envy, greed, and lust. The gray mist of secularism stupefies the sense of holiness, stifles moral outrage, intimidates ethical indignation, questions the worth of purity. Godliness is gone as a virtue; evil seems respectable. In the words of Barbara Nauer, it has become good to be bad.[3]

Modern learning is powerless to challenge this beguiling mood, for its humanistic and naturalistic temper make it part of the problem. Most college classrooms now deny God equal or any time and disavow the idea of his rewarding good and punishing evil. Positivistic anthropology equalizes the values of all cultures, and process theology declares that all that happens is streaked with divinity, while scientism can validate no moral norms whatever.

Most persons are oblivious to how fixed moral values are menaced by the growing notion that a truly democratic society must allow, even requires, ethical diversity and a tolerance of immorality. Those who promote this theory argue that moral judgments are a private matter only, that an emphasis on ethics in public affairs represses democratic attitudes and processes, and that ethical absolutism is the handmaid of totalitarianism.

Unless we challenge the prejudices of social theorists for whom the cultural consensus alone dictates public policy, we shall soon preside over the collapse of democracy into chaos. This modern appeal for empirically derived "group values" easily snared mediating theologians who had abandoned divinely revealed commands and moral principles. Evangelical Christians ought to be the first to insist on the existence of ethical absolutes and their applicability to national life. They know that an empirical approach cannot identify absolutes and that Christ, who will judge the nations for their disregard of the revealed will of God, is in fact judging them even now in anticipation of that coming endtime.

Humanists may deplore this emphasis as an attempt to restore the Hebrew theocracy; modernists will resist an espousal of positions other than their own as an imposition of evangelical establishment prejudices. Something much deeper is at stake however; namely, the current entrenchment of moral pluralism as a social norm. American society is being conditioned by the dogma that democracy requires ethical diversity and that the inherited biblical morality must therefore be transcended. The next step will be to insist that all moral distinctions are relative.

Our Christian duty includes a public proclamation of the standards by which the Coming King will judge all men and nations. If Christ's church does not publicize the criteria by which Christ will judge the world, how will the world know them? Whatever legislation a pluralistic society may approve, Christians must not aid and abet the notion that public policy respecting abortion, homosexuality, prostitution, marriage and divorce, poverty, or anything else is answerable only to pragmatic consensus concerning the good.

If Christians are to be politically relevant they must, to be sure, support truly viable legislative options (even if such options are less than ideal and may require early revision). In rare circumstances will they be called upon to challenge the divinely intended "God-state" of Romans 13 for acting like the "Beast-state" of Revelation 13 where the saints prepare for martyrdom. This side of the millennium all civil governments will be less than ideal, and politically active Christians should not be misled into seeing themselves as bringing in the kingdom of God. The gospel is not identifiable with whether one is pro or con French-speaking Quebec or pro or con SALT II. Different persons may draw somewhat different inferences from biblical principles and even take opposing political sides on some issues. But no basis exists for dividing the church as a body over political particularities that Scripture does not require or prohibit.

Yet the evangel has obvious implications for public life and public affairs. Confident that God works providentially in the history of nations and that we are to seek a good conscience in fulfilling our duties, we should feel impelled to greater responsibility. If Christians fully recover and carefully balance their evangelistic mandate and their public duty, they may help turn the rumors of endtime into the realities of springtime. God calls the church to be literally the new society, a brotherhood with a mission in the world, a beacon of hope amid human misery, a society that exhibits life in true community. But we must not confuse evangelistic proclamation of voluntary grace with legislative compulsion of public justice. To seek all ends by politics is as wrong as to seek all ends by evangelism. The apostle Paul appealed to Caesar to repudiate the misguided heirs of the theocracy; it would be worse to appeal to the theocracy to repudiate Caesar. Jesus knew the tension in human life between the claims of love and justice; that same tension will encompass Christians until the Lord returns and swords are beaten into plowshares.

The God of the Bible challenges our ready confusion of the biblical heritage with the enthusiasms of civil religion. He disputes the sentimental view of our nation as an extension of the kingdom of God, bewails our failure to confront public conscience by the biblical criteria of morality and justice, and mourns our collapse of Christian conviction into expedient political alternatives. For a century ideologists have made the poor and the oppressed their battle cry even while the plight of these souls has worsened. To say that "rich Christians" hold the solution to this tragedy is an exaggeration. But if, unlike the Bible, we never excoriate profligate politicians or the greedy or the worldly wise, is it because we secretly have too much in common with them, or because we enjoy the status symbols of a disordered society, or because we spend too little time in the company of Jesus? God is calling evangelical Christians to a deep and dedicated commitment to humanity at large and to the true welfare of man, to friendship with the poor, to a fulness of love and action that will not freeze in winter, to a lifestyle that includes self-denial and sacrifice.

Occupy till I come, said Jesus. A church unoccupied with the right priorities will soon become preoccupied with the wrong priorities. Watergate prosecutor Leon Jaworski, who had also been chief prosecutor for the Nazi war crimes trials, tells us in his auto-biography that when Christians in the land of Luther—"seemingly God-fearing, well-meaning humans"—neglected church relation-ships, they eagerly gave themselves to Nazi nationalism and de-teriorated into "vicious beasts." Moral decay in America, Jaworski warns, could spread like a cancerous growth. "The Church militant is the only antidote," he declares, and emphasizes that "without a militant membership . . . the church cannot fulfill the God-given responsibilities."[4] *Occupy till I come*—that is Jesus' word to us.

THE DAY OF THE LORD

Finally, in addition to occupying, Jesus exhorts us to *be ready*. The parable of the nobleman's far journey ends with his re-turn, but the parable of the one who comes like a household thief begins with the householder's sudden return. The intervening period until the Lord's return coincides with the age of missionary outreach. First, said Jesus, the gospel of the kingdom would be "preached in the whole world as a testimony to all nations, and then the end will come" (Matthew 24:14). *Be ready!*

In our materialistic age of scientific advance and moral de-cline, multitudes of people protect their possessions behind triple locks and costly security systems. No society in history has so lived in constant fear of the household thief as does modern America. There is no reason or excuse, therefore, to miss the point of Jesus' warning. "Therefore keep watch, because you do not know on what day your Lord will come. . . . If the owner of the house had known at what time of night the thief was coming, he would have kept watch. . . . So you also must be ready, because the Son of Man will come at an hour when you do not expect him" (Matthew 24:42, 43, 44).

Paul repeats the admonition in his very first letter: "The day of the Lord will come like a thief in the night" (1 Thessalonians 5:2). Peter echoes it in his last letter: "The day of the Lord will come like a thief" (2 Peter 3:10). John solemnly refers to it in the Apocalypse: "Behold, I come like a thief! Blessed is he who stays awake" (Revelation 16:15); "But if you do not wake up, I will come like a thief, and you will not know at what time I will come to you" (Revelation 3:3). *Be ready!*

Our interim age is not open-ended; it carries an expiration date. We are to ready ourselves not only for Christ's return but also for a new beginning with its manifested glory and power. *Be ready!* The regenerate church is the only Body of Humanity that Christ will welcome into the eternal order. The Risen Head, from whom the Body draws its life, is already seated on the Father's right hand. Through the Spirit he already imparts to the Body, as a sample of our inheritance, some of the powers and virtues that characterize the coming age.

Just as secular society would strip supernatural creation and the redemptive miracles of their credibility, so recent views of science and history would strip eschatology also of credibility. Inflexible mathematical sequences were imposed upon the world a century ago. Timid existentialists in our century translated creation and eschatology into internal divine-human encounters. The currently most influential view is the humanist theory that projects an inherently unpatterned and chaotic universe whose only order and meaning is imposed upon it by human beings.

Those who ask no eschatological questions because they think the divine answering service is dead are in for a surprise. There is hard news ahead for those who regard inflation or sexual impotence or communist expansion as the most frightening thing in life. While eschatology is good news for the Christian, it is a doomsday message for the rebellious and ungodly. God, the pure Light, who shines in our hearts in salvation, will also render the rebellious and renegade visible for what they truly are. Human history moves toward a far worse fate than that of ancient Pompeii; Mount St. Helens's ashes strewn over proud modern cities are but a deft suggestion of the coming fury. *Be ready!*

Not long ago fire gutted the Las Vegas Hilton, America's largest and the world's second largest hotel. While many guests on upper floors perished in the flames, others in the hotel casino below disregarded the sirens and blithely continued to gamble. No odds can justify a gamble on eschatology. Jesus says, *Be ready!*

No one can negotiate or determine his or her rites of passage into the world to come. On the judgment seat, at the portal between this life and the next, is one whose hands have borne for two thousand years the uncomely nailprints of crucifixion. His eyes are "like blazing fire" (Revelation 1:14). "Behold . . . every eye will see him, every one who pierced him; and all tribes of the earth will wail on account of him" (Revelation 1:7, RSV). All nations—united nations and divided nations, developed nations and developing nations, free world nations and totalitarian nations—will gather for judgment before the Coming King. All races—black, brown, yellow, red, and white—will be held accountable for their doing or undoing of God's will. Christ the Risen Lord will vindicate the good and the godly.

Today so much sensational literature, so much eschatological conjecture confuses churchgoers that they are prone to ask the experts for a second opinion. Some practitioners chart a detailed system of prophetic details filled out by weekly newspaper headlines. Others care only about the caboose that follows fast on the long train of redemptive events and stand ready to pull the emergency brake when they suspect everyone should jump.

For Paul and the other apostles, Christ's second coming is the heart of the future: the resurrection of the dead, the final judgment with its reward of God's people and doom of the wicked, the new heavens and new earth. I agree with those who insist that the Book of Revelation centers not in dates or places but in the risen and returning Lord, in the Lamb slain for sinners from the foundation of the world, in the One sovereign over space and time. The kerygma or apostolic core-message gives us, no less than the early Christians, the best perspective for preaching on the edges of eternity. It emphasizes Christ's incarnation, sinless life, substitutionary death, bodily resurrection, personal return in judgment of men and nations, and his glorious kingdom.

At the outset I said something about explaining the universe and giving several examples. No generation has manipulated the universe more astonishingly than ours: atomic energy and the doom of Nagasaki and Hiroshima, space travel to the moon, unparalleled medical advance alongside the wanton destruction of millions of fetuses annually, and now the age of computer science.

Theology sets before us several universes—the one God created, the one man despoils, the future new heavens and earth over which Christ shall reign. We may yet decide, if we press the alternatives, that ours is not the best of all possible worlds; that the best life is one made ready for the world to come.

"I am come" . . . "my church" . . . "Scripture cannot be broken" . . . "occupy" . . . "be ready!" These themes take us from here to eternity. Even on a drab day, they enable us to see forever.

"Theology for Our Day," Notes

1. Sheldon Vanauken, "The English Channel," *New Oxford Review,* March 1981, p. 11.

2. Harry Blamires, *Where Do We Stand? An Examination of the Christ's Position in the Modern World* (Ann Arbor, Mich.: Servant Books, 1980).

3. Barbara Nauer, "The Face of Evil on Bourbon Street," *New Oxford Review,* January-February 1981, pp. 9-13.

4. Leon Jaworski, *Crossroads* (Elgin, Ill.: David C. Cook Publishing Co., 1981), p. 208.

Evangelism: Looking Back and Looking Ahead

Whether one speaks of evangelism yesterday or of evangelism tomorrow, nothing should deter us from this God-entrusted task, for our planet is strafed by unrest and strife and world leaders are confused and unsure. Vast multitudes find life bitter and bewildering—without Christ they are eternally doomed.

Not long ago I met for two days with a dozen evangelical leaders, some of whom have ready access to Capitol Hill. Our national policymakers wrestle constantly with aimlessness and directionlessness in political affairs and cope with often unforeseeable events that seem beyond human control or solution. The evident need is for a new vision of God: of his governance in the fortunes of nations and of his personal blessing on those who love and serve him.

The present world predicament would not have surprised Jesus and the apostles, and it should not surprise us. Of almost four billion people, three billion are not Christians; two-thirds of the earth's population have not even heard the gospel. Every one of the

This address was first presented on 23 February 1982 in Oak Park, Illinois, at the twentieth anniversary evangelism conference sponsored by Northern Baptist Theological Seminary and other American Baptist agencies.

nearly 150 million who are born each year needs to hear about Christ and his salvation. More and more the world interprets redemption only in political and economic terms, a misunderstanding sadly encouraged primarily by Western influences. Our own nation faces an acute crisis of soul in material and moral and spiritual matters.

We parry detailed questions about the possible end of the world while millions around us are dying morally and spiritually. Beleaguered by indelicacy and indecency, by tastelessness and vulgarity, our sophisticated society is given on the one hand to a hatred of ultimate truth and on the other to irrational passion. There is little remembrance of a long-gone age when the calm reflection of a reasoned existence prevailed. The only way to change one's mind, it would seem, is to see a psychiatrist.

Skepticism, caricature, and ridicule of the gospel abound. Secularism is no less hard-core than pornography. From the decadence of our times there is no place to go but hell, unless repentant man takes hold of God by the ankles and clings fast.

OPPORTUNITIES FOR EVANGELISM

Despite the moral and spiritual gloom of our times, Christians have every reason for hope and high courage. Why should we allow the world to cast its pall upon us? No segment of humanity has more joy, more moral power, more inner peace, more enduring hope for the future than those of every race and nation who have come to know Christ. It is high-opportunity time for a bold sharing of good news.

This period in history is, in fact, the new "third age of missions" in which the Christian task force is deployed worldwide in the media and space age. Twenty centuries after Christ came in the flesh and half way around the world, the gospel reached you and me in a multitude of different contexts and circumstances. Now, for the first time, there are Christian believers in every land on the face of the earth—some underground, some in tentmaking ministries, many with an unimpeded witness. Yesterday's age of the great missionary pioneers was followed by the age of global expansion. Today is the age of international deployment. What tomorrow will be depends upon what we do with it. Today a billion pagans live in areas where Christians speak their languages and have existing churches. Were we to seize the opportunities of the space and media age the other two billion could be reached. One reason why the Baptist theologian Josef Ton welcomed his eviction from Rumania is the opportunity afforded by the free world to transmit the gospel by radio to those whom communism would deprive of it.

Not only has the third age of missions dawned, but longtime "receiving" churches are now becoming "sending" churches. Third world churches are taking proper pride in missionary engagement; their growing zeal gives fresh impetus to Western Christians. Nowhere is this evangelistic boldness more evident than in Korea, where believers determined not only to double the number of Christians in their homeland before its 1984 centennial of Protestant missions, but also to send workers to other parts of Asia and to other continents as well. Thousands of Korean high school and university students have volunteered a year of evangelistic service wherever and whenever God opens a door.

If we leave world evangelization only to the professionals, global evangelism will contract and diminish. The obstacles to worldwide endeavor are in part tactical: 85 percent of the Third World, for example, is closed to traditional foreign missions. There are also organizational hindrances. Once on the field, workers are usually so burdened with multiple responsibilities that far too little time remains for soul-winning. There are obviously also financial obstacles. The 1980 international congress in Pattaya, Thailand, estimated that two hundred thousand missionaries are needed if we are to complete the global task of evangelization in our century. Can we reasonably expect to rally that many fulltime workers, raise $6 billion for their support (at a modest $28,000 per family), put them through language school, and transport them to the field?

Besides enlisting competent professional missionaries we need urgently to recover "the missionary nature of the congregation," an emphasis widely neglected in our lifetime. The secret of

Protestant expansion in Latin America has been not a clergy financed by a middle class to carry on an evangelistic witness, but a working class that reaches out in love to families, friends, and fellow workers. While God has certainly used them, the evangelistic task by and large is not to be implemented mainly by jet-conditioned itinerants and professional verbalizers.

Tentmaking ministries are gaining new emphasis as Christian workers abroad share their faith on the margin of their daily work. Writing out of long experience in Afghanistan, Christy Wilson, in his book by that title, sees tentmaking as the key to missions in mainland China. Such evangelistic witness may not be under board appointment but it is nonetheless by appointment of the King. Consultants and technicians, teachers, students, and other workers can bear a natural witness in the world of work. We can be grateful that on the American scene there have emerged special movements like Christian Medical Society, Christian Legal Society, and most recently the acceleration of prison ministry through the conversion of Chuck Colson.

SOME THOUGHTS ON METHODOLOGY

We evangelicals are keenly interested in new methods of evangelism. In workshops at the American Festival of Evangelism held recently hundreds of new ideas were shared. Two observations, however, bear special emphasis.

First, *every method of not evangelizing is wrong*. Some methods surely are better than others, some more appropriate than others in different circumstances. There is room for a vast variety of techniques and procedures without absolutizing any, among them the "four spiritual laws," Evangelism Explosion, and one-on-one discipleship. Some have become institutionalized, none is beyond improving, and each has facilitated evangelistic outreach. Yet we need to avoid millennial expectations and the blatant triumphalism that overstates our parochial successes as if they were more than models and that represents our momentary victories as if they were decisive conquests of the world-spirit. People were won to Christ in the past by other methods. Even from a timid gulp in an emotion-streaked testimony God can still get glory.

A great debate is being waged today over the electronic church. Skepticism over television evangelism springs in part from media newscasters who market only this world's bad news and who often doubt the existence of any ultimately good news. Some criticism comes from established denominations that resent the competitive financial appeals and the prospect of rival local parachurches linked as informal congregations to remote evangelizers. Some criticism is surely drawn by the TV evangelists themselves due to the amount of time they spend in direct and indirect promotion and fundraising, and the substance or style of their presentation. Yet the fact is that eighty million Americans remain uncommitted to any organized faith, and many who tune to these religious programs hunger for a personal faith and have not been otherwise reached. If time spent in criticism were devoted instead to evangelizing the nation by a better use of the media, we would earn our right to criticize and set ahead the neglected mission of the church.

Second, *the best method is,* always has been, and always will be *person-to-person evangelism.* Even in our century this approach holds the best promise of evangelizing the world. If one in four of the world's four billion inhabitants is listed by statisticians as a follower of Jesus, then is it not high time for those who expect truly to be counted as Christians to speak to neighbors and townspeople about Christ? How many would fail the test, and how often, if in each Sunday service those were asked to stand who during the past week had witnessed to one person about Jesus Christ? Will professing evangelicals come to grips with the sin of silence about the Savior? This question is far more important than such queries as whether mass crusades are at their end, whether radio evangelism has a future, whether the electronic church will soon fade away. Only divine omniscience can assuredly decide those issues.

W. Stanley Mooneyham says quite rightly that "world evangelism is too big a task to be left to an elite." Senate Chaplain Richard Halverson stresses that God has dispersed Christians as his ambassadors throughout the nations to witness to the lost; he has put us where we are in our work for the sake of testimony to Christ.

The more than ten thousand persons attending the recent American Festival of Evangelism vowed in the next year to win one hundred thousand persons to Christ. Are we ourselves making the effort?

THE CRUCIAL ROLE OF THE LOCAL CHURCH

The local church—right where you are—is a crucial link in fulfilling this task. Parachurch movements have made an amazing impact in our time, largely because major denominations have neglected or have been unable to fulfill vital aspects of their mission. But revival has almost always begun in the local church, not in parachurch movements or in denominational headquarters. Renewal of the local congregation is vitally important for the evangelistic task.

Even where only a minority of their members have become evangelistically active, local churches show evident growth. The fast-growing Coral Ridge Presbyterian Church in Fort Lauderdale at one stage listed only 15 percent of its members in its evangelistic vanguard.

Women still far outnumber men as members and workers. Jesus Christ is Lord of the sexes—where are the men hiding? Someone has called them "the church's overlooked minority." Christ is calling tax collectors and tentmakers and doctors; where are the modern Matthews and Pauls and Lukes? In our American churches, many need the spiritual regeneration that precedes evangelistic motivation.

Let the world see that God is alive and at work in our local congregations. To many observers institutional Christianity seems to be decadent. Even so detached a critic as Malcolm Muggeridge says "organized religion kills the living beauty of God."[1] Has the church lost all concern for discipline? Not even worldlings respect a church that harbors immorality. The time has come to break with compromised moral convictions, to challenge professing believers who are halfhearted about fixed ethical principles and who commit themselves instead to what they call near-chastity. Our bold talk about reforming culture means nothing apart from an inner transformation of individuals who evidence personal piety and godliness. Without spiritual renewal evangelism is a mockery to the Lord.

I spent my early years as a newspaper reporter and editor before I became a Christian. From a journalist's viewpoint I was perplexed that after his resurrection, the most striking event in human history, Jesus should restrain his disciples from witnessing to the world at once and should insist instead that they wait, wait, wait until the Holy Spirit had empowered them: "Stay in the city. . . . you will receive power . . . and you will be my witnesses" (Luke 24:49; Acts 1:8). One needs to learn that the divine resources are as important as the human; indeed, they must have the preeminence.

Episcopal rector William H. Swatos, Jr., writes of the declining fortunes of "denominational religiosity" and notes that nondenominational churches are emerging as "local equivalents of the traditional denominations."[2] The trouble with the traditional denominations, says Swatos, was that they were swamped by sociocultural conformity, emphasized religious pluralism, and overlooked the importance of voluntary commitment. In short, the big denominations while trying to survive as distinctive local groups minimized their distinctives at the national level. Their most active local churches meanwhile preferred to become evangelical first and Baptist, Methodist, or Presbyterian only secondarily. The hierarchies had little ground for complaint, however, since they wanted their churches to be nationally pluralistic and only secondarily denominational.

This evangelical orientation of the local churches is nurtured not only by a desire for biblical roots, but by a conviction also that in its congregational ministry the local church should address the problems of the community. Key '73 was perhaps ahead of its time when it proposed that in every city and village evangelical believers, irrespective of denominational and ecumenical affiliation or nonaffiliation, stand in an arm-to-arm witness to the entire community of the joy of a personal relationship to the Redeemer and to the rewards of Bible study. That same cooperative effort could in time have fashioned also a common local protest against grievous community injustice and might have projected ethical alternatives.

A thoroughly powerful evangelistic message must now be 'holistic'; that is, it must address the plight of the whole man in his total predicament. Many churchgoers seek out local ministries that address the community in its comprehensive context and mirror Christian concern for man's complete need. Evangelicals have made the turn to social concern. Most evangelicals are rediscovering social involvement to be a necessary task and are responding in a larger way to man's physical needs.

What evangelicals now need to distinguish is what belongs properly to evangelism and compassion and what belongs properly to legislation and coercion. Having done so, we then need to render to God what is God's and to Caesar what is Caesar's.

While government cannot save America, we nonetheless can't do without it. Only proper priorities can keep government from becoming totalitarian or chaotic, however, or from lapsing into intermediate corruptions.

Social action per se cannot save the American soul. Western religious voices who tell us that we cannot effectively speak to the Orient in its need unless we redistribute our material possessions need to hear Eastern religious voices who travel to the West's spiritual vacuum and blame Western materialism for our plight. Reshuffling and relocating materialism will simply substitute new victims for the present ones.

Nor can technology per se save America. Only biblical values can keep nuclear power from destroying civilization, keep genetic manipulation from desecrating the creation, or keep a generation hypnotized by the pagan icon of television from imposing its profane fantasies upon the social order.

The Necessity of Theological Renewal

Evangelism will limp along, moreover, in the absence of theological renewal. Nothing blunts the evangelistic edge more than the unbiblical notion that everybody will surely be redeemed or, what comes to much the same thing, that nobody needs to be redeemed. Prominent academicians have promoted universalism, among them C. H. Dodd, Nels Ferre, Paul Tillich, and, despite his best intentions, even Karl Barth. Yet the apostle Paul's message reflects an unyielding conviction that without faith in Christ human beings are lost and that they need everywhere to hear and believe in him of whom they have not heard (Romans 10:13-17). Important as are the social implications and imperatives of the gospel, the now vague and ambivalent term "mission" must be defined to preserve what the apostle considered of first importance—that Christ died for our sins and lives to give new life to the spiritually dead. The sense of doomsday evaporates where religionists forfeit the conviction that human beings are spiritually lost. Do we retain a deep awareness that judgment is lowering over our fellow Americans and over our nation? Is there no Noah among us who daily hammers home to our townspeople the message "repent, *repent,* REPENT!" while the ark rises for whosoever will? Despite all the good things we may say about our own most-favored country, national and individual judgment are both near.

Let me stay a moment longer with the subject of theological renewal. A least-common-denominator evangelism soon becomes a no-denominator evangelism. I can't vouch for the figures; in fact, I sincerely hope they are wrong. But one writer recently said that 95 percent of the members of evangelical churches in the United States would fail a biblical literacy test. In the mid-South a religion department chairman tells me that students enroll in university Bible survey courses to learn belatedly what they should have gotten in their local churches. At the American Festival of Evangelism, the booth manned by Paulist Fathers announced openly its interest in promoting traditional Romanism rather than evangelical Catholicism. Much evangelical evangelism is so theologically thin that it invites nonevangelicals to provide a blood transfusion.

I agree with that now deceased giant of the pulpit Martyn Lloyd-Jones, G. Campbell Morgan's successor at Westminster Chapel, that evangelical evangelism now focuses so one-sidedly on the new birth—absolutely necessary though it is—that it often obscures the substitutionary death of Christ for sinners as the ground of our salvation. We need to revive the tradition of great and powerful doctrinal preaching—to recover the themes of divine creation, revelation, providence, resurrection, and judgment to come.

We must not simply verbalize the truth, to be sure, but insist that God's truth calls for an enfleshment in life; the truth is to be "done," as John the evangelist states (John 3:21), and not simply to be "known." At the bottom of racism, of materialism, of infidelity and the breakup of the home, is a disavowal of biblical truth and values.

But biblical values have a short-lived and short-changed existence where people surrender the supernatural and defect from God revealed in his holy Word. Personal piety will not long survive the loss of the living God who claims all creation as his domain. So burdened was apostolic Christianity with the task of identifying Jesus the Messiah to both Jews and Gentiles that it found little opportunity to emphasize the failure of secular philosophy, that is, of world-wisdom. Yet the apostles believed and proclaimed the unity of truth. They heralded Christianity as a personal faith, but they affirmed its validity also in every arena of thought and life. They knew, of course, that Greek and Roman philosophy were not the ultimate source of human unbelief; they knew revolt against God to be far older than the Ionian philosophers and Democritus. The impetus to unbelief they found, not in man's changing systems of thought or in his social environment, but in the fallen nature of man in revolt against his Maker. At the bottom of that revolt lay a perverse will given over to misconceptions of the authority of the Creator and of God as the Lord of truth and the good.

But we must spend more time exhibiting the superiorities of the biblical worldview and proclaiming the victories of the gospel than in exposing the vanities of our generation. The 1990s will judge us more for what we do to win our contemporaries than for the correctness of our intellectual and social analyses. Awake we must to factors that we may easily overlook even in a time of limited spiritual resurgence, to developments that could adversely affect the spiritual climate of America, to tendencies that call for response and action.

SPECIAL OPPORTUNITIES FOR EVANGELISM

Let me suggest some special targets for American evangelism, opportunities that may all too easily be lost, factors whose neglect will be costly not only for the church but also for the nation and the world.

Influx of Hispanics

Immigration has added four hundred thousand persons a year to the nation's population; beyond that there are now three to six million illegal immigrants. Many seek only materialistic betterment and bring a religious formalism devoid of any vital personal faith. By the year 1990 Hispanics will be the largest minority in the United States. We need, therefore, to undergird a comprehensive national mission led by Spanish-speaking evangelicals and to take larger interest in literacy programs. Multitudes of us—I among them—are evangelical converts reared in the homes of American immigrants.

Growth of Nonbiblical Religions

Adherents of non-Christian religions have been entering America in unprecedented numbers, many of them as refugees from Indochina and other lands. The altered religious balances in England hold instructive lessons for us. There are now in England almost a million Muslims and a quarter million Hindus. There are more than two hundred mosques, some of them stately and impressive structures. Two churches have closed for every mosque that has opened; some so-called redundant churches have actually reopened as Hindu temples. William Carey said, "Expect great things from God; attempt great things for God." What would he say today to the Christians of Leicester where in the name of urban renewal the city has torn down the building where Carey received his call and where the church that sent him to India has become a Hindu temple? There are already, I am told, three hundred Muslim mosques in America and increasing numbers of Buddhist gatherings and Hindu services. Home missions has indeed become foreign missions.

We have only ourselves to blame if we do not enlist the thousands of American evangelicals who are vital Christian converts from Oriental religions. They know best what misery their former religions still perpetuate in Asian lands. They represent a vital avenue of witness to their transplanted compatriots about the God of the Bible. In Washington the religion page of the *Post* advertises meetings for Bahais, Scientologists, Spiritualists, and Swamis. A colossal Mormon temple in nearby Maryland mirrors the increasing strength of the cults. Given their present growth rate, there will be twenty million Mormons in the United States by the end of the twentieth century—more adherents than Southern Baptists or Methodists. Has the time not come for a massive and constructive witness to adherents of the nonbiblical religions and the subbiblical cults?

Ministry to Foreign Students

In 1980 our universities and colleges enrolled 264,000 foreign students; by 1990, it is estimated, foreign students will comprise about 10 percent of the entire collegiate enrollment. Most of these select students come from Third World countries to which they will return as future leaders. Many of these young people have very loose ties to their inherited religions. They are infatuated with technological science; along with technology, American education most influentially exposes them to secular humanism as a worldview. The Christian outreach to these students is sporadic and highly limited, although some are curious about Christianity and at times open to it. International Students carries on a ministry among foreign college students through small Bible studies, periodic retreats, and friendship evangelism. Youth for Understanding arranges lodgings in homes for high school students from Europe and Latin America, and attracts evangelical families as hosts. What are we doing to lift the minds of this vast audience of young intellectuals to the profounder vistas of truth and reality in a land where thirty million adults profess to be evangelical Christians?

SOME RELATED CONCERNS

At least three concerns on the edge of evangelism will help change the tone of our witness: religious liberty, response to university learning, and evangelical deathstyle.

Religious Freedom

In eliciting human decision for Christ we should emphasize that religious freedom is the ideal context in which human beings make their spiritual commitments. An earthly society in which man is free to choose atheism is better than one in which he is compelled to choose theism. To witness to the world of many religions that Christianity has the least to fear—and indeed nothing to fear— from universal freedom to adopt any religion (and therefore promotes freedom to worship the true God in good conscience), carries its own important message in a day when communists require atheism, Muslims prohibit conversion under penalty of death, Israelis restrict evangelism, and even some Christians display religious intolerance. The best way to compete with imposed religion or with imposed irreligion is to herald the news that true religion insists on freedom to choose or to reject beliefs in good conscience, and that individuals are ultimately responsible for the personal decisions they make. In an age of totalitarian tyrants and religious despots, the evangelical should be perceived not simply as the promoter of a particular religious, ethical, or political agenda but first and foremost as the champion of human liberty.

University Learning

Over twelve million persons are attending U.S. colleges and universities, many on campuses where classrooms now predominately echo a naturalistic philosophy, often in the form of secular humanism. This interposes a massive barrier to the intellectual credibility of supernatural theism. For multitudes of students religion is irrelevant. Despite these contrary pressures, the gospel has confounded many professors by reaching around the classroom into the lives of tens of thousands of students who have emerged as the most vigorous evangelical vanguard in the Christian churches.

There is nonetheless a great failure to battle for the intellect and to dispute secular humanism, an internally inconsistent and reductionist theory of reality, one that God in his revelation expressly repudiates. Neither the seminaries nor the evangelical colleges have shaped a pertinent literature that boldly and powerfully addresses the secular learning that governs the mood of the age. This nonfulfillment of an academic responsibility needlessly accommodates the tide of philosophical hostility toward biblical theism. The present mood of the campus is antiintellectual, to be sure; students absorb nonbiblical teaching not so much to appropriate it as to take a raincheck on inherited beliefs. Only 10 percent of the students on many campuses are academically serious students; among evangelical students, unfortunately, the number is probably less rather than more. In many places, moreover, the nonintellectual mood has been remedied little by either Campus Crusade or Inter-Varsity Christian Fellowship. Never have there been so many wasted young minds and rootless intellects. Some of our prestigious universities first arose in order to equip leaders to preach the gospel. We must take more seriously the liberating significance of Jesus for the intellectual. In a world of learning that wallows in beggarly excuses for unbelief we once again must set forth a mind-stretching theology and adduce sound reason for our hope.

Evangelical Deathstyle

We usually think in terms of a ministry to the dying; let me speak instead of ministry by the dying. Paul writes of the early Christians as "dying, and yet we live" (2 Corinthians 6:9); we are therefore all of us the dying, and Christian lifestyle and Christian deathstyle concern every one of us. Evangelical deathstyle can in our generation be as important as evangelical lifestyle for the cause of evangelism.

A few years ago I heard of one Christian lady who during her terminal illness made hospital appointments with each of her neighbors and with other townspeople to share with them the consolation of a vital faith in Christ and her living hope of the afterlife. Many professedly religious people pass out of this life into the next with no confident hope much as do worldlings. To go into the Lord's presence soon after sharing salvation's joy with a neighbor, who remains to relay the good news to others, may be high heaven's grand witness that the biggest legacy the people of God leave to fellow mortals is the open secret of knowing Jesus.

"Evangelism," Notes

1. Ian Hunter, *Malcolm Muggeridge: A Life* (Nashville: Thomas Nelson Publishers, 1980), p. 47.

2. William H. Swatos, Jr., "Beyond Denominationalism," *Journal for the Scientific Study of Religion* 20 (September 1981): 217-27.

Religious Freedom: Cornerstone of Human Rights

A Timely Concern

*F*or the first time in the history of the nations and of the churches of Christendom there exists today a universal verbal consensus in support of the principle of religious liberty.

This consensus is the flowering of a long and arduous process of debate and reflection. In pre-Christian times all societies were sacral and bound by a common religious and political loyalty. Religious freedom was first extended by Christian and by Muslim nations to pilgrims in transit to Palestine; later many nations extended it also to foreigners engaged in navigation and commerce. The Protestant Reformation enabled princes to choose their own religion, yet their subjects were expected to adopt the ruler's faith or to move to a territory where a preferred faith was established. The protection afforded early Mennonites, however, anticipated a widening tolerance. Baptists insistently voiced an accelerating call for religious minority rights.

This address was first presented on 10 July 1983 at the conference on Religious Freedom East and West: The Human Rights Issue for the Eighties. This conference was sponsored by the Institute on Religion and Democracy and by the National Association of Evangelicals and was held in Washington, D. C.

The United States Constitution broke new ground. It refused to leave religious liberty concerns and other human rights to determination by the majority. The First Amendment stipulated that "Congress shall make no law respecting an establishment of religion, or prohibiting the free exercise thereof." In 1948 the concept of freedom of religion was embraced in the United Nations Universal Declaration of Human Rights.

Despite the verbal affirmation of religious liberty in international and ecclesiastical documents, most societies and an incredibly large number of human beings still do not possess it. United Nations signatory states are, moreover, unable to agree on a common definition of religious freedom. The subsequent Helsinki Declaration of 1975 espouses the principle that, alone or together, individuals are free to profess and practice religion or religious convictions according to the dictates of conscience. Yet the document reserves internal jurisdiction to each state to interpret this principle in its own way. Radical thinkers redefine it to mean something that generations before Freud and Marx would have found unthinkable, that religion is a product of neurosis and that deliverance from neurosis entails freedom from religion.

Today, religious freedom is bartered not only by totalitarian rulers seeking to advance official atheism, but by Free World leaders as well who adjust human rights considerations to military and economic priorities. The time is highly propitious, therefore, for a renewed focus on religious liberty concerns.

Despite the impressive verbal support for religious liberty, no consensus exists on its theological or sociological basis. The crisis touching religious freedom therefore runs much deeper than its atheistic totalitarian repression and its restriction by authoritarian and by insistently theistic nations.

My thesis is fourfold: first, that biblical theism alone provides adequate intellectual struts for a meaningful doctrine of religious liberty and for other human rights, while nontheistic views render such rights merely postulatory and problematical; second, that religious liberty as a universal human right is appropriate and indispensable to human beings irrespective of creed; third, that the right of religious freedom in fact shelters and nurtures all other human rights; and finally, that evangelicals who value human freedoms as the gift of the Creator, whom we seek in good conscience to worship and serve, should engage more actively in championing religious freedom everywhere as well as in promoting the religious freedom of Christians in secular American society.

THE BASIS FOR RELIGIOUS LIBERTY AND HUMAN RIGHTS

Serious discussion of religious freedom begins with the recognition of religious freedom as a basic human right, a right whose suppression strips away essential components of human dignity. Religious liberty is not mere religious tolerance, suspended as that is upon the arbitrary will of rulers. If religious freedom is advocated only for pragmatic reasons, it can and will be sacrificed to expediency.

Modern secular scholars depict supernatural religion as hostile to human rights in view of epochs of intolerance and inquisition. But the most vicious assault on human rights has been inspired by naturalistic philosophies such as Nazi socialism and Russian and Chinese Marxism. The most brutal repression of human rights and maltreatment of human beings has been implemented by movements launched by foes of biblical theism. Some of these foes have been foremost among those who misrepresent revealed religion as hostile to human rights.

Western humanists, to be sure, champion human rights. They do so even though humanism as a philosophy provides no metaphysical basis adequate to preserve those rights in distinction from other principles that humanism relegates to a sociocultural by-product of a particular period of history. Universal and permanent human rights are logically inconsistent with the humanist theses that personality is an accident in the universe and that human nature is evolving. We cannot empirically extrapolate unchanging values and final truths either from a world of impersonal processes or merely from the human situation. I commend humanists who promote human rights, even if they wholly lack a consistent philosophical basis for justifying them. Far better were they to connect their social agenda with an overarching theistic worldview able to support an absolute standard of rights and fixed ethical imperatives.

On the basis of God's scripturally revealed purpose, evangelical Christians affirm values that transcend all human cultures and societies and human rights constituting the norms of civilization. Objectively grounded human rights are logically defensible on this foundation of the supernatural creation of man with a unique universal dignity. It is no accident that much of the rest of the world overlooked rights recognized in the biblically enlightened West, and that early leaders of the modern human rights cause were influenced by the Decalogue and the biblical doctrine of human dignity.

Secular philosophy today not only is incapable of defending human rights but, in the absence of absolute values, it increasingly also encroaches upon and erodes them by a selective reduction of human value and worth. So, for example, in sexual ethics, the rights of fetal life are neglected while those of homosexuals are energetically pursued.

The historical connection between revealed religion and freedom has nonetheless been disconcertingly ambiguous. Theists have not always championed religious liberty as they ought. Leo Pfeffer even holds that "compulsion in religion is a heritage of the monotheistic worship which Moses commanded must, under penalty of death, be accorded to a jealous God."[1] But much as the Hebrews protected their religious heritage against alien influences, they did not compel Gentiles throughout the Near East to adopt revelatory monotheism; in fact, they lacked missionary passion. While death was the stipulated penalty in the Old Testament theocracy for anyone in the Hebrew community who departed from strict monotheism (Deuteronomy 13:6-11; Leviticus 24:15-16), the New Testament by contrast presupposes pluralistic nations in which state and church occupy different spheres of influence and fulfill different functions under the one sovereign will of God. The state is not to be the servant of the church nor is the church to be the servant of the state. In New Testament perspective the state serves a limited function; it is not to be the source and stipulator of human liberties. Rather it is to preserve and promote divinely given rights in a political framework of justice and order, enabling human beings to voluntarily do what God requires.

Yet Constantinian Christianity, as we are painfully aware, enthroned the confessional state and repressed any threat to imperial and ecclesial unity. Christianity and Islam as well as socialism and communism have as historical phenomena sponsored pernicious religious repression. Not until post-Reformation Christianity in sixteenth century Holland was religious tolerance extended to Anabaptists, Jews, and people of other faiths. And it is only fair to concede that evangelical Christians have not in the recent past been the active vanguard of human rights concerns, including religious liberty issues. They have neither aggressively condemned rights violations nor aggressively championed the preservation of rights except when and as their own interest has been involved. Some evangelicals, worse yet, have dismissed the concern for rights as an irrelevance or as an unnecessary detraction from evangelistic priorities. A few have even given the impression that the redeemed people of God inherit rights that mankind generally lacks or has forfeited. The historical situation invites the reactionary view that an ideal society, defined as essentially humanistic, requires the subordination of church, synagogue, and mosque.

Yet a necessary link exists between Judeo-Christian faith and human freedom, as we have indicated, since biblical beliefs best anchor and illumine the values essential to social well-being. The evangelical view is that human rights are grounded in the revealed will of God, that religious liberty and political liberty are alike based on the Bible. The attempt to ground human rights other than theologically cannot effectively sustain itself. The crucial issue therefore arises whether religious freedom, properly understood, requires freedom *from God* or freedom *for God,* freedom from man or freedom under God for man, freedom from conscience or freedom for conscience.

A major weakness of the United Nations Universal Declaration of Human Rights adopted in 1948 was and is its failure to clarify the source and sanction of human rights that signatory powers are required to honor. Since all particular states are called upon to give constitutional guarantees of these rights, the individual states cannot themselves be the source of these rights but rather are answerable for preserving them. Yet the U.N. Declaration does not identify the transcendent source of rights. It leaves unstated whether or not a *super*state—perhaps the United Nations itself—might ultimately be viewed as the source and stipulator of human rights. Were Marxist or other totalitarian powers to dominate the United Nations, could they then manipulate the content of human rights on the premise that all particular nations are answerable to the catalogue of rights that this international or supernational body imposes? That eventuality would not only render the content of human rights fluid, it would also suspend it on the whim of totalitarian rulers.

The American charter documents made explicit what the U.N. Declaration later obscured: that God the transcendent Creator is the source and ground of human rights, and that human beings universally bear these rights by virtue of divine creation. The Declaration of Independence expressly affirms human rights on the ground of the sovereign creative act of the moral Maker of mankind. All men, it states plainly, are "endowed by their Creator" with certain inalienable rights. This transcendent theological referent excludes the legitimacy of any tyrannical suspension of human rights and instead requires the state to recognize universally given prerogatives that belong as a supernatural endowment to the dignity of the human person.

RELIGIOUS LIBERTY A UNIVERSAL RIGHT

The U.N. Declaration in 1948 included religious freedom as part of its agenda of human rights. It affirmed that "Everyone has the right to freedom of thought, conscience and religion; this right includes freedom to change his religion or belief, and freedom either alone or in community with others and in public or private, to manifest his religion or belief in teaching, practice, worship and observance." Since some religiously specific nations rule out changing one's religion under risk of death or exclusion from the community and restrict the right to pursue evangelism, this affirmation is doubly important. The right was transformed into a legal obligation for ratifying states in 1966 by the International Covenant on Civil and Political Rights whose Article 18 affirms everyone's "freedom to have or to adopt a religion or belief of his choice."

Subsequent Muslim pressures, however, precipitated a revision. When the U.N. Declaration on the elimination of religious discrimination was approved in November 1981 (after twenty years of committee work), references were deleted to the right "to adopt" (and hence "to change") one's religion and only the right "to have" a religion was retained. Article 1 consequently reads that "the right to freedom of thought, conscience and religion . . . shall include freedom to have a religion." The final article in the 1981 Declaration does affirm that nothing therein is to be construed as restricting any right defined in the 1948 Declaration or in the 1966 International Covenant, but it is disappointingly weaker as a document on religious liberty.

The 1966 International Covenant and the 1981 Declaration, moreover, blur the sense of religious freedom by perpetuating the confusing reference in the 1948 Declaration to freedom of "religion or belief." The meaning of religion is itself widely in debate. Recent philosophers such as Paul Tillich equate the religious referent with whatever is man's object of "ultimate concern" (and atheism is the ultimate concern of some contemporaries). Freedom of religion, therefore, is here rendered ambiguous. Some would accordingly ground religious liberty only in a respect for the vast multiplicity of human faiths and beliefs or even base it on skepticism over the possibility of arriving at truth of any kind.

My point is not that religious liberty should be withheld from those whose beliefs we find radically objectionable or whose beliefs may diametrically oppose our own. But it does no service to the cause of religious freedom to assume that the term "religion" (or "religious") has a universally agreed content. Anything and everything from devil worship to human sacrifice has been commended as religion. Either by religion we designate specific religions or we designate nothing specific at all. Freedom does not establish human existence as a self-enclosed life without moral norms and duties. Either human rights and liberties have a fixed and definable content that excludes alternatives, or human rights include the right to dehumanize human nature and religious freedom becomes freedom for its contradiction and negation. If one infringes the rights of others or endangers the morals of others in the name of religious liberty, liberty becomes irresponsibility. Religious freedom is not a rubric that licenses liberty to do anything and everything in the name of religion. Either the Ten Commandments provide a divine prototype of enduring rights or religious liberty consists ultimately in freedom from God.

This is not to deny that religious freedom is an unconditional civil or legal right. No finite agency has the right to invade man's inner spiritual life. No corporate authority, whether ecclesial or political, can be considered absolute since the sinfulness of humanity permeates even social bureaucracies. Human beings have in respect to religious concerns a right to immunity from coercion in civil society.

In view of this the effort of ecclesial majorities to influence governments not to grant religious freedom to those of other persuasions and to preserve a privileged role for themselves has in recent times been aggressively challenged. Even where the constitutions of some nations still give special legal recognition to the Church of Rome, the civil right of religious liberty is now acknowledged. Concordats with Argentina, Portugal, and Spain, for example, have been modified in the interest of civil religious freedom.

To affirm civil religious liberty, however, one need not presuppose that human beings have an intrinsic right to religious liberty, or even that an individual's religious beliefs and commitments should be free from either ecclesiastical or parental coercion. What we are due as citizens need not coincide with what ecclesiastical bodies hold is due us in other relationships. Vatican II (1962-65) did not affirm religious liberty as a right fundamental to human dignity and universally intrinsic to human personhood, a right shared by all human beings irrespective of their religion or lack of it. Instead, it acknowledged only what scholars call a "negative right," that is, the right of immunity from religious coercion. The encyclical *Dignitatis Humanae* (1965) implies that every human person has a private realm and inner relationships in which he must individually and responsibly decide matters of religious reality and truth.

Yet *Dignitatis Humanae* refused to separate discussion of religious freedom from the question of religious duty on the ground that privilege inescapably implies responsibility. Every person has the right to immunity both from coercion to act against conscience and from impediment against acting according to conscience. Not a single human thought or act, therefore, is exempt from conscience. In short, everyone has a right to do one's religious duty to worship God as conscience dictates. Vatican II moreover resisted the widespread modern notion that all religions are of equal worth. But it did not recognize any right of those holding other religions to propagate error.

The interrelation of religious freedom and conscience remains one of the most important and difficult facets of religious liberty discussion. Religious freedom is not unconditional in the sense of dissolving the obligation to be true to one's conscience. That human beings knowingly and universally do act contrary to conscience is a basic emphasis of the Christian doctrine of the sinfulness of mankind. But the right to act according to conscience is recognized, for example, in the recent provision for pacifists of alternatives to military service. But to act according to conscience is not necessarily to perform good acts. Public expressions of conscience are not wholly exempt from legal penalties.

The traditional Roman Catholic emphasis on religious tolerance implied that the church should feel humane understanding toward those who in good faith and conscience profess religions that the church considers false. Such understanding did not, notably, involve any acknowledgement of the right of those professing another religion to proclaim and promulgate it. In recent decades, however, the Church of Rome has supplemented this traditional emphasis on humane understanding by an additional emphasis on respect for others irrespective of the content of their religious beliefs. In December 1976, Pope Paul VI declared that religious freedom is "intimately linked with the dignity and the personal dynamisms of man."[2]

Freedom of conscience means that those committed to other faiths and those claiming to be committed to none must not only be respected but also accorded equal rights. Yet this is not to affirm the inviolable sacredness of human conscience, for in that case no distinction can be made between good and bad conscience. An inner compulsion to do what is immoral cannot be defended in the name of human rights or duties, not even in the name of religious freedom. When polygamy was banned earlier in this century, the prohibition turned on what—contrary to Mormonism—was perceived by the rest of American society as immoral. The Hindu practice of suttee (the immolation of a widow on the funeral pyre of her husband) is now forbidden. Human conscience is fallible; it needs correction and guidance by a transcendent norm. More specifically, it needs to be informed by the Word of God.

The reason no one should be compelled to act contrary to conscience is not that conscience is always right but that no divine or good power motivates one to act against conscience. The apostolic imperative was not simply to "obey conscience rather than men" but to "obey God rather than men" (Acts 5:29). In short, religious liberty shelters liberty of conscience in that man is ultimately responsible not to his fellow men but to God for the decisions he makes and the options he pursues. The apostles say nothing about an absolute or wholly unqualified right to repudiate God. What they recognize is that man chooses whom he will serve and bears the consequences of such decision not as determined by state or society but by the final judgment of God. The will of God constitutes the ultimate justification of religious voluntarism. A mechanically imposed faith is not genuine faith; a coerced commitment has value neither to God nor to man.

RELIGIOUS FREEDOM ESSENTIAL TO ALL OTHER RIGHTS

Religious liberty is not only a fundamental human right, but it shelters also the whole broad spectrum of human rights. It is the mainspring of freedom. The right to worship and serve the true and living God carries with it all the divinely vouchsafed rights and duties. Religious liberty involves much more than the right to hold one's faith and to express it both in worship and practice, to propagate the gospel and to persuade and teach others, and to give religious education to one's children. It embraces also the right to peaceful assembly and association, freedom of opinion and expression, freedom from arbitrary arrest and detention, and freedom to leave one's country and to return. Deprivation of such rights impairs religious freedom. If curtailment of one's political and civil liberties rightly raises anxieties about religious liberty, curtailment of one's religious liberty inevitably prepares the way for many strictures on political and civil liberty. Freedom is comprehensive and indivisible in principle; it cannot be fragmented without jeopardy to the whole.

Thus the whole bastion of universal rights and duties rests, in a double sense, upon a theological basis. Although the U.N. Declaration (1948) did not address the question of the interdependence of human rights, the priority of religious liberty has during the past generation gained increasing recognition. Paul VI remarked that among fundamental human rights "religious liberty occupies a place of primary importance."[3] The statement of the central committee of the World Council of Churches (Chichester, 1949) is even more pointed: "Religious freedom is the condition and guarantee of all true freedom." The Bible grounds true freedom at every level expressly in God: Israel's deliverance from totalitarian pagan enslavement is God's free choice; civil government is divinely ordained to maintain a free course for justice and order (Romans 13:3-5); Christ Jesus frees humans enslaved to sin (John 8:36); and the creation itself will one day be set free supernaturally for the liberty for which it now yearns (Romans 8:20-22).

Despite international covenants that complement and supplement the U.N. Declaration, religious intolerance continues in many countries. Although totalitarian regimes active in the United Nations legally recognize the right of religious freedom, such governments are among the first to abridge it and to substitute in its place religious tolerance suspended upon the will of the state. The political tolerance level varies from totalitarian state to totalitarian state, but restriction runs the gamut from official efforts to destroy religion to discrimination against those who personally cling to religious faith. Despite constitutional guarantees, totalitarian countries repeatedly violate assurances of religious freedom even while they seek to persuade the outside world that religious rights are respected. States whose official philosophy is atheistic routinely practice religious intolerance. The fact that Marxist persecution often strengthens religious commitment and purifies religious belief spurs the totalitarian bureaucracies to greater refinement of their systematic and sporadic restrictions on religious freedom.

No governments have been as inhumanely intolerant as the Nazi socialist regime in Hitler's Germany and the communist regimes in Stalin's Russia and Mao's China. Post-Mao China, for the moment at least, seems to be relaxing religious intolerance more than post-Stalin Russia, Bulgaria, and Rumania. After President Carter raised the subject of China's resistance to the importation of Bibles, Vice Premier Deng Xiaoping in 1981 initiated a constitutional amendment guaranteeing freedom of worship, although China's official policy remains the abolition of religion. While atheistic states acknowledge the freedom of individuals to hold any religious commitment privately, they seriously restrict the right of individuals to publicly express or practice religious beliefs and their implications. Both in Russia and in China the communist regimes approve a progovernment ecclesial agency to negotiate with all churches. Groups that seek to preserve their independence have difficulty functioning legally and are suspected of being unpatriotic and in league with foreign powers.

In the Soviet Union, Christian, Jewish, and Muslim religious leaders remain in prison, unfree to teach their religious convictions in their own country. One Free World agency, CREED, has a caseload of almost a hundred persecuted Russian Christians for whom it intercedes. It took nearly five years in the basement of the American embassy, where they sought refuge after serving discriminatory sentences to prison and labor camps, for the Siberian Pentecostals to receive Soviet permission to emigrate. Observance of prescribed rituals has been impeded, religious teaching curtailed, church properties taken over or restricted in use, publication and distribution of religious literature hindered or prohibited. KGB officials have disguised themselves as secret carriers of scarce religious literature to gain entry into Christian homes; once literature was accepted and stored police conducted house searches and placed the occupants under arrest. Wives and mothers and friends of imprisoned Christian workers have been arrested and fined for gathering to pray for the release of prisoners.

In Rumania restrictions on trained pastors are such that some Baptist clergy serve a dozen churches. Not only printing of religious literature but even its duplication by typewriter is impeded. Recently three hundred Baptists had to align themselves between their local church and bulldozers to keep city officials in Iasi from leveling it. After it had been damaged in a 1977 earthquake, government officials for the next five years refused to grant permission for needed repairs and then tried to demolish it.

The right of religious freedom clearly has immense political significance. For it affirms a fundamental sphere of life in which civil government has neither divine authority nor human competence to act. In the last analysis political liberty and restraints on government alike rest on the sovereign God who has published his will in Scripture and in conscience. Duties to God are not to be invoked to undermine the state's legitimate authority, nor are the state's political powers to be deployed either to prohibit or to propagate religion. Neither on the ground of race, color, religion, culture, nor political conviction are human beings to be deprived of religious liberty or of the other human rights it shelters.

In recent years social revolutionaries have confused and clouded the understanding of religious liberty by invoking it against governments hostile to churchmen who demand swift and radical political alternatives. Special concern for the exploited and oppressed was indeed a hallmark of the biblical prophet; nowhere does the passion for individual worth and social justice run deeper than in the Judeo-Christian Scriptures. But the authentically biblical character of political concern is rendered problematic when its ecclesial champions approve violence and fund and promote revolutionary means for achieving social change. It is equally problematic when they tie their call for justice to Marxist analysis and solutions. An essentially politico-economic program—one that lacks sound biblical supports at that—is then advanced under the banner of religious liberty despite the fact that sociohistorical implementation of Marxist ideology has notably impeded religious freedom and suspended human rights on the will of the ruling class. Religious freedom does indeed include, as the World Council of Churches Fifth Assembly in Nairobi put it, "the right and duty of religious bodies to criticize the ruling powers when necessary" on the basis of religious principles. But politicization of the church's message should not be sanctified as indispensable to the preservation of religious liberty.

Ecumenical leaders acknowledge subtle and important shifts in the World Council's orientation of religious liberty as proposals for economic change and altered social structures were advanced under this canopy. As national sociopolitical changes were comprehended as aspects of the gospel, a program that had earlier been assimilated to human rights discussion generally was now linked expressly to religious liberty. Political activities were thereby declared religious; coercive and revolutionary overthrow of social structures in a Marxist direction became biblical rebellion and was promoted as an implementation of human rights and, more expressly, as a matter of religious freedom. The discussion of individual rights was transmuted into a question of collective rights with the objective of implementing new social structures. Criticism was concentrated more on the deficiencies of the Western democracies than on repression-laden totalitarian lands. Clearly, not all politico-economic criticism that rises from religious conviction should be taken uncritically as an authentic expression of religious freedom concerns.

My observation is not intended to excuse or to gloss human rights violations in dictatorial societies hostile to communism or in democratic societies that also need more fully to implement the rights they affirm. Human rights infractions should be protested wherever they occur; indeed, no earthly paradise of fully achieved human duties and rights anywhere exists.

The fact that the United States has economic ties to Saudi Arabia, military pacts with Turkey, and deep links to Israel in the interest of stability in the Near East is no reason for ignoring vital religious liberty concerns in those countries. Most Muslim lands provide little or no freedom to change one's religion. In Saudi Arabia and in Turkey it is almost impossible to establish a church even for expatriots. In Indonesia, where many Muslims have become Christian, the legislature has banned the works of a Christian author who responded to publications that distort and attack Christianity.

The Israeli Knesset currently is formulating a human rights policy. The proclamation of Israel's independence in 1948 gave assurance that the state of Israel "will guarantee freedom of religion, conscience, education and culture, will safeguard the Holy Place of all religions, and will loyally uphold the principles of the United Nations Charter." Unlike Islamic countries in the Middle East which declare Islam to be the state religion, Israel does not make Judaism the religion of the state; Israeli leaders characterize the state as Jewish only in an ethnic or national sense. Israel permits the entrance of missionaries in numbers proportionate to the size of their existing ecclesial constituencies and encourages dialogue in place of normal missionary effort. The government, in fact, pays the salaries of Christian and Islamic clergy on a proportionate basis.

In 1977 the Knesset, after some clamor for an antimissionary law, adopted an anti-enticement law with steep penalties for any donor or recipient. The minister of justice, defending the law on the ground that the Holocaust has precipitated "a natural desire to see to it that no people will be lost in the Jewish faith in an undue and unjustified process," denies that its intention was to impede "normal educational and philanthropic activities."

Ugly incidents, largely on the part of Orthodox Israelis who also protest the secular character of the state, sporadically exhibit religious hostility to Christians. Such incidents have included damage to church properties, destruction of the First Baptist Church of Jerusalem by arson, and disruption of a performance of Handel's Messiah (in this case by a Mormon choir). Outbursts by extremists must be distinguished from government policy, but unless they are boldly challenged by those who approve government policy, that policy is easily weakened for the sake of political considerations. American Jewish leaders quickly and commendably joined Christians in expressing dismay to the Israeli ministry of religion.

AN EVANGELICAL AGENDA FOR PROMOTING RELIGIOUS FREEDOMS

I offer in conclusion five brief observations focusing religious liberty concerns in evangelical perspective.

Government Encroachment on Freedom

We must be alert to government encroachment upon religious freedom in America no less than elsewhere. Among the critical issues we face are: public school exclusion of a forefront emphasis of the nation's charter political documents—that is, the supernatural creation of man with divinely endowed inalienable rights; discrimination against religious speech in voluntary meetings on public school campuses; the state's redefinition of the legitimate scope of church ministry so that religious schools, orphanages, and nursing homes (activities that churches conducted long before government awakened to them) must comply to government requirements not merely in matters of health and safety but also philosophically; and finally, a denigration of the meaning and value of human life through legalization of abortion-on-demand.

Obligation to Civil Laws

At the same time religious movements must not misuse or exploit public institutions for religious ends. Religious liberty involves specific responsibilities of the churches and other religious movements not only to society but also to the state. Church bodies are obliged to keep the civil laws. Exceptions to this obligation do occur, however, when the governing regime is notoriously corrupt and itself subverts the norms of civilized society or when those laws contravene conscience. In the latter case, dissenters should inform the authorities and be ready to suffer the consequences rather than to try to circumvent them.

The courts properly investigate the sincerity with which beliefs are held and the propriety with which they are applied. In the name of Islamic religion Muslims put to death members of their own family if they defect to atheism or convert to a non-Islamic religion; Jonestown approved mass murder; others fund violence as a means of social improvement. There is legitimacy in the requirement that leaders of religious movements respect crime laws, in the exclusion of essentially political activity from nontaxable religious ministry, and in the taxation of churches for related business income. When Jonestown became a base for Marxism it became susceptible to government investigation and exposures; its murder-suicide of over nine hundred members of Jim Jones's People's Temple was evidence that investigation came too late.

Religious Freedom for All

We must earnestly protect the religious freedom of all who come to our shores, be they Christian, Jewish, Muslim, Buddhist, Hindu, Confucian, or whatever—even while we passionately proclaim to all the gospel of Christ. Religion that can perpetuate itself only by depriving others of liberty is not worth having. An evangelical faith is truly strong if and when it becomes a symbol of freedom of religious belief to those who even in this twentieth century face death because of human rights violations or who rot in prison because they would live in good conscience. Voluntary religion, unaligned with a confessional state and unsupported by public taxation, has enabled American evangelicals to number fifty-five million and to help extend Christianity worldwide as the first living faith with a global presence. We must assure those who come with other faiths, even those that disallow their adherents to change their religion, that we have nothing to fear from a society in which all are free to worship God as they will. Further, we shall help to preserve for all who come to America the right in good conscience to change their religion if they aspire to do so or to worship if they so prefer in the tradition of their fathers. "Choose for yourselves this day whom you will serve" (Joshua 24:15) is as appropriate and indispensable to evangelical proclamation as is "you must be born again" (John 3:7).

Jewish–Christian Alliance

We face a specially opportune moment, I think, for American Jews and evangelical Christians to forge an exemplary alliance that puts principle above propaganda, makes a common stand against religious intolerance at home and abroad, and yet fully sustains the freedom to promulgate religious beliefs and to evangelize. European Jews were once great believers in the tolerant pluralistic state; America as a pluralistic nation has been a land of religious freedom for Jew and Christian alike. Instead of silence when Christians misread the violence of fanatics as official attempts to eliminate a Christian presence in Israel, or when Jews brand American evangelistic efforts as expressions of anti-Semitism, let us be counted on the side of truth and liberty. For we know that Messiah at his coming will judge us all by the light we have had and that in the present civilizational darkness freedom of religion is a bright beacon of promise.

Secularist–Christian Alliance

In that same spirit I extend a hand also to humanists and others who, even if their alien and contrabiblical philosophies seem to many of us unpromising, nonetheless would share in the defense and promotion of authentic human rights in a bleak age of totalitarian tyranny. It is not the role of government to judge between rival systems of metaphysics and to legislate one among others. Rather government's role is to protect and preserve a free course for its constitutional guarantees.

"Religious Freedom," Notes

1. Leo Pfeffer, *Church, State and Freedom* (Boston: Beacon Press, 1953).

2. *Osservatore Romano,* 9-10 December 1976.

3. *Evangelii Nuntiandi,* 8 December 1975, n. 30.

The Crisis of Modern Learning

THE DRIFT OF MODERN LEARNING

*T*he most sudden and sweeping upheaval in beliefs and values has taken place in this century. No generation in the history of human thought has seen such swift and radical inversion of ideas and ideals as in our lifetime.

At the outset of this century the instructional program of the great Western universities frequently referred to the God of the Bible, the living self-revealing God. Courses in moral philosophy gave prominence to the Ten Commandments and to the Sermon on the Mount, and presented Jesus of Nazareth as the perfect example of morality. Studies in social philosophy stressed that for history to attain a utopian future some change in man's inner disposition or character is necessary, if not because of original sin (which was increasingly questioned on evolutionary assumptions) then at least because of man's supposed inheritance of brute propensities and animal instincts.

This address was first presented on 18 September 1983 at Hillsdale College, Michigan, at the opening of the Christian Studies Convocation sponsored by the Center for Constructive Alternatives. It was also published in the February 1984 issue of Imprimis, *a publication of Hillsdale College.*

By the late 1920s a striking shift of perspective had prevailed. References to deity no longer focused on the God of Abraham, Isaac, and Jacob, the self-revelatory God of biblical theism, but rather on an anonymous God-in-general, a John Doe god. God was now inferred from the not-God. Philosophers of religion argued from the existence of the cosmos to a divine Cause, or from the design of nature or pattern of history to a divine Designer, or from human conscience to a divine Lawgiver, or from the mind of man to an Absolute Reason. Instead of the One God there emerged varieties of gods, both infinite and finite, personal and impersonal—even growing gods. Naturalists, meanwhile, dismissed God entirely except as but a convenient symbol for man's supreme social or private values. Little agreement over the nature of deity survived even among philosophers who considered metaphysics their special province. Faced by this vanishing theoretical consensus, American educators abandoned the concept of God as the integrating factor in modern university learning.

Instead of God, shared moral values became the cohesive force in liberal arts studies. This emphasis on ethical norms was not, however, associated with biblical imperatives and divinely revealed commandments. The study of morals was increasingly pursued independently of theological concerns. (Some campuses nonetheless scheduled annual "spiritual emphasis" weeks, not unmindful of promotional and funding benefits amid waning if not already severed denominational ties.) Man's distinctive nature, it was said, requires a hierarchy of values that subordinates material realities to ethical duties; these ethical duties, however, may or may not in turn require spiritual or theological illumination.

The shift of educational perspective concerned not only the vision of God and of moral imperatives, but also the nature of the dawning future and the means of implementing utopia. No longer was an internal change in man's nature or character considered necessary, and especially not the supernatural regeneration of fallen man on which Christian theism insisted. Instead education, politicization, and socialization of the human race were to be the catalysts of a new age. Western learning would be carried to the ends of the earth, democratic ideals would be exported to all the nations, and the realities of human brotherhood in one world would facilitate the triumph of universal peace and justice.

Today much of that kind of thinking is gone.

No significant place remains for God or the gods in the university classroom. Courses in science and in history dismiss deity as irrelevant. Psychology texts usually introduce God only as a psychic aberration. Even some religion departments still rumor the "death of God." Philosophy departments are in the grip of post-positivistic analysis and tend to sidestep supernatural concerns; others disown the supernatural and creatively restructure ultimate reality. Over against most departments where both the God of the Bible and the John Doe god are now shunned as extraneous, the literature department alone seems at least to reflect the great theological concerns in a literary context.

In the absence of unrevisable absolutes, universities vainly expected that common values would nonetheless integrate modern learning. What we actually have is a normless tolerance of diversity, of deviation which is linked with a democratic outlook and often with respect for minorities; moral absolutes are associated only with totalitarian bureaucracies. A relativistic morality given to self-assertion lampoons the truth that tolerance without norms destroys even tolerance and that democracy without norms invites chaos.

Not only have the pluralistic gods and shared moral values become pale ghosts of the campus, but confidence has broken down as well in education and politics as dynamic catalysts of social change. Instead of reliance on orderly means of social change, including respect for law and deference to established conventions, the mood of contemporary social transformers is increasingly open to revolutionary coercion and violence as the preferred alternatives that assure rapid and radical alteration.

Meanwhile education itself succumbs to pressures to curtail the humanities, a course of action that would even more abridge the already reduced common intellectual experience of students. These pressures come not only from the physical sciences, which are now the indispensable core of modern learning, but also from the vocational needs of students. They come no less from a sense that academe has lost intellectual excitement and reward. The liberal arts have impoverished themselves by their neglect of enduring spiritual concerns and by their studied exclusion of Judeo-Christian perspective in a radically secular age.

The drift of twentieth century learning can be succinctly summarized in one statement: Instead of recognizing Yahweh as the source and stipulator of truth and the good, contemporary thought reduces all reality to impersonal processes and events, and insists that man himself creatively imposes upon the cosmos and upon history the only values that they will ever bear. This dethronement of God and enthronement of man as lord of the universe, this eclipse of the supernatural and exaggeration of the natural, has precipitated an intellectual and moral crisis that escorts Western civilization, despite its brilliant technological achievements, ever nearer to anguished collapse and atheistic suffocation.

THE AFFIRMATIONS OF MODERN LEARNING

The shaping ideas of contemporary university learning can be readily identified. Its key concepts are dependency, transiency, relativity, and autonomy. These terms have always had a proper place in the explanation of man and the world, and all the more so in a generation that knows the space-time universe to be immensely older and immensely larger than even our grandparents suspected. But what distinguishes the modern view is its antitheological and antisupernatural stance. The modern view affirms *diffuse* dependency, *total* transiency, *radical* relativity, and *absolute* autonomy.

In affirming the independence of God, classic education denied the comprehensive contingency of all reality: the Creator of the universe has the ground of his being in himself, whereas the universe in its totality is dependent upon its Maker and is pervasively contingent. The current view, by contrast, depicts all reality as a matrix of contingency; it reduces all existence ultimately to nature in some form, that is, to physical processes and events.

Earlier education affirmed, further, the reality of an eternal spiritual and moral world grounded in the supernatural being of

God; it denied that reality is completely in the clutch of time. By contrast the current view affirms the transiency of the whole of existence. The biblical conception of an eternal Logos who shaped all worlds it considers mythology and without explanatory importance. All that exists, we are told, bears an expiration date; man and beast alike move toward death as their final destiny.

Earlier education affirmed that truth and the good are fixed and final; it denied that right and wrong are culture-relative. The current view, on the other hand, asserts that all ideas and ideals are relative to culture—all ethical imperatives, all philosophical pronouncements, all theological doctrines are partisan prejudices of the sociocultural matrix. It rejects outright eternal and revealed truths, divinely given commandments, unrevisable religious doctrines.

Given this emphasis on the culture-relativity of truth, certain other tenets of the current view seem somewhat arbitrary (for example, its confident dogmas of complete contingency and total transiency). The fact is, a consistent espousal of culture-relativity would lead not to such speculative finalities but to skepticism, since pervasive dependency and total transiency would be doctrines rooted in our own particular cultural perspective.

But the current view also affirms, and aggressively so, the absolute autonomy of man. Its test of whether modern man has truly "come of age" turns on whether one repudiates all eternal, objective, and transcendent authority, and affirms instead the ultimacy of personal decision and creative selfhood. Man is considered his own lord in the area of truth and morals; the only values that the cosmos and history will ever bear, in the current view, are those that man himself insinuates into the course of events.

For more than a decade these premises—diffuse dependency, total transiency, radical relativity, and absolute autonomy—have dominated the university classroom more influentially than any and all other alternatives. They have become the masked metaphysics, the covert conceptuality of modern liberal learning. Almost every sampling of student reaction to liberal arts studies in the mainstream colleges and universities in the last decade evokes the overwhelming verdict that these students considered themselves intellectually constrained to shape their worldview by these controlling emphases.

This naturalist outlook notably differs from the atheistic communist view only in secondary details rather than in basic assumptions. The official teaching of communism is that nature and history are objectively structured by a pattern of economic determinism, a determinism that assures the ultimate triumph of the proletariat. Free world naturalism, by contrast, views this claim as pure mythology and considers nature and history instead to be intrinsically unpatterned. But both perspectives are equally anti-theological, both repudiate a divinely given truth and morality, and both reject a supernatural purpose in nature and history. While communism views the state as the authoritative stipulator of truth and right for the collectivity of mankind, Free World naturalism on the other hand elevates creative individual selfhood.

It is a fact, of course, that the present student generation is less idea-oriented than job-oriented. Some reports estimate the number of seriously intellectual students at only 10 percent. Some improvement is underway as women students aspire to careers in medicine, law, and other professions long dominated by men. As other coveted vocational opportunities presuppose academic competence serious students competing for scholarships are once again returning to long-forsaken libraries. Scholars who consciously accept the naturalistic worldview are frequently encouraged by their mentors to pursue graduate studies and to become university teachers.

Among most students, the pressures of naturalistic theory serve actually to dull the force of the inherited Judeo-Christian view or at very least to postpone individual commitment to its high moral and spiritual demands. The emergence of selfism or a *me*-first outlook on life is resisted most strenuously by that minority of students who, against the winds of modernity, maintain vital ties to orthodox Judaism, Catholicism, or evangelical Protestantism. The overall impact of recent liberal arts studies has been to seal off the spiritual world, however, and to concentrate classroom interest on changing space-time tentativities.

THE ATTRACTION TO HUMANISM

What specially attracts liberal arts students to naturalism is its emergence in the form of humanism, a philosophic system that adds to the naturalistic agenda a program of social ethics. Humanism emphasizes not only man's duties to his fellow man and to nature, but also certain expectations from his fellow man and from nature. Human beings, we are told, ought to champion social justice, promote human rights and racial equality, and be concerned about poverty. They ought, moreover, to preserve natural resources and avoid polluting the cosmos. Humanism also emphasizes certain human expectations from nature, which is assumed somehow to uphold personal worth and security. Although most secularists abandon any expectation of individual immortality, some have assigned their bodies to deep freeze at death in the hope that science in the next century will be able to retrieve them for endless life on earth.

This correlation of a humanist agenda of social ethics with a naturalistic worldview has been attacked from right and left as a philosophical monstrosity that defies logical consistency. A system that denies that personality has decisive significance in the origin of the universe and considers personality but an accidental by-product of blind and unthinking forces can hardly affirm that nature specially defers to man or that man is bound by enduring duties. The consistent outcome of naturalistic theory is not a special status for mankind but the essential purposelessness and meaninglessness of human existence.

The inconsistency of the humanist is perhaps most apparent in his response when he is wronged by a fellow human being. If a humanist professor at State University were to park his new Jaguar and discover upon returning that an unknown driver had done massive damage to the side of his car, he would predictably not offer a public eulogy to the latest defector from objective values who, having emerged from ethical adolescence, now considered all ethical imperatives culture-relative and creative selfhood to be decisive for morality. Far from it. He would, instead, suddenly inherit a vocabulary with eschatological overtones that his naturalistic metaphysics does not logically accommodate.

From the right—that is, from the side of biblical theism—the humanist emphasis on social ethics has long been assailed as a borrowed fragment of the Judeo-Christian heritage which it was unable completely to disavow. Christian theism by contrast affirms not only a program of social ethics but also an agenda of personal ethics. Moreover, it insists that love for God holds priority over love for neighbor and for self. Modern secular philosophy, as D. Elton Trueblood contended, promoted a "cut-flower civilization," one destined to wither because severed from its biblical roots. In addition, it presented only preferred remnants of the Judeo-Christian moral imperative.

Evangelical criticism of the humanist program was not, however, a powerful intellectual classroom force. Only a minority boldly voiced its claims against the counterpressures of comprehensive naturalism. Evangelicals, moreover, were themselves embarrassed by propagandistic fundamentalist claims that humanists, in view of their atheism and tolerance of deviant lifestyles, were the enemies of morality.

More recently, however, criticism of the illogic of humanism has proceeded increasingly from the left. Radical students who identify themselves with the naturalistic worldview have pressed university professors to defend their espousal of "conventional morality" in the realm of social ethics given the controlling tenets on which humanism rests. As Karl Löwith remarks, naturalism provides no real basis for man to feel "at home" amid statistical averages in a universe born of an explosion. One can go further. Naturalism provides no objective basis for moral obligation, no basis for expecting that the cosmos will specially cater to man. The governing principles of comprehensive contingency, total transiency, and radical relativity can accommodate no special meaning and worth for human existence. A cosmos in which personhood emerges only as an oddity and as an accident cannot sustain as its primary value an agenda of man's objective duties to nature or to his fellow beings. The consistent implication of naturalism is that man does not matter and that nature has no special place for personality. Naturalistic evolution can sustain neither the universal nor the permanent dignity of man.

The humanist modification of naturalism to accommodate an agenda of social ethics is evidence enough that while naturalism as a metaphysical system is thinkable, it is not humanly livable. Naturalism dissolves the worth and meaning of human survival. The naturalist postulates one set of ideas theoretically; the humanist adjusts them experientially and existentially to contrary expectations from nature and man.

TENSIONS WITHIN HUMANISM

I have noted cardinal assumptions of the modern worldview and indicated that humanism modifies the naturalistic mindset by illogically appending an agenda of social ethics and insisting on the special value of man. The reason for this deviation, however inconsistent with the basic beliefs of naturalism, is not a matter simply of illogic. Nor is this compromise due only to sentimentality, that is, to an inability of humanists, contrary to hard-core naturalists, to divest themselves wholly of inherited Judeo-Christian precepts. Humanism does accommodate fragments of conventional morality that naturalism in principle excludes.

What needs specially to be stressed, however, is that the reason humanism adjusts naturalistic beliefs experientially to universal ethical imperatives is that like every other human being the humanist is related to a larger realm of being and life and value, one that he neither creates nor controls. He cannot wholly escape God in his revelation nor wholly suppress the claim of the *imago Dei* upon his psyche. He is informed about inescapable moral obligation far more than the naturalistic theory implies. The New Testament clearly affirms that the Logos of God lights every man (John 1:9) and that the revelation of the Creator penetrates to the very being of even those who would suppress or excise that disclosure (Romans 1:18-32; 2:14-15). Despite his intellectual and moral revolt against the supernatural, fallen man is unable to fully free himself of God's counterclaim upon his mind and conscience.

Secular man vetoes God's claim intellectually and by his own theoretical postulations renders that claim personally powerless.

But he does not thereby cancel or destroy that claim, nor can he wholly escape it. His very compromise of the naturalistic world-view shows that theoretical atheism is inadequate to explain the totality of existence. The humanist is torn between contrary demands: while his radically secular theory renders supernatural claims ridiculous and irrelevant, his moral and ontological claims about man and society actually link man responsibly to God in his revelation. On a naturalistic basis he cannot consistently mount a persuasive case for ethical imperatives. What stimulates him to moral concern is the inescapable general revelation of God and the ineradicable image of God which, however sullied by sin, survives in man as the imperishable gift of the Creator.

The humanist perspective, therefore, is nurtured in part by hidden resources. At the crucial point of the nature and destiny of man, the humanist forsakes the consistent demands of naturalism and incorporates instead alternatives that only a theistic view can coherently and adequately sustain. The Bible clearly illumines the tension that besets the humanist's refusal to opt either for thoroughgoing naturalism or for thoroughgoing theism. On the one hand, the universal general revelation of God, in which the humanist shares, explains his concessions and departures from a consistent naturalistic account of man and the world; on the other, spiritual rebellion or sin explains his theoretical exclusion of the supernatural. The humanist seeks to suppress God's claim but cannot wholly eradicate it. Like all other human beings he stands perpetually related to God in his self-disclosure and cannot totally obscure the *imago Dei* that by creation stamps man with special dignity and worth.

A Spiritual Resurgence

Given the intellectual dominance of naturalism in the contemporary university, one would expect that if ever a student generation were to be wholly lost to a supernatural faith—and especially to the Judeo-Christian heritage with its distinctive revelatory claim—the present collegiate masses would be doomed to that fate. Yet it is one thing to say that on balance the university classroom most influentially promulgates the view that impersonal processes and events comprise the ultimately real world, and quite another to say that atheistic naturalism, whether humanist or non-humanist, has captured the student mind.

While most students, even many who pursue studies in philosophy, delay any serious wrestling with metaphysical concerns, there are tens of thousands in the American evangelical movement whose personal faith in Christ and commitment to Christian theism dates back to high school and university. Their exposure to Judeo-Christian realities came not in connection with classroom studies but mainly on the margin of formal studies, through association with fellow students whose devotional vitality and moral dedication contrasted notably with the spiritual apathy and ethical permissiveness prevalent on the secular campus.

In large part ecumenical student activity had waned because of concessions to the speculative climate. Doctrinal and evangelistic concerns were replaced by radical sociopolitical protest. Evangelical movements such as Inter-Varsity Christian Fellowship, Campus Crusade for Christ, Young Life, and The Navigators left their mark despite contrary academic pressures. Such evangelical efforts were largely experience centered, although Inter-Varsity in America, like its British counterpart, engaged increasingly in the publication of books that enlisted the student mind. But even on mainstream secular campuses, scores and then hundreds of students emerged to witness that they had found the crucified and risen Christ a living reality and now treasured the Bible as God's written Word. Like Augustine they declared that the presuppositions of secular philosophy are not necessarily infallible, and with disarming confidence they spoke of supernatural realities and staked their lives on the eternal verities. Like C. S. Lewis, they affirmed that one can be "surprised by joy" in an intellectual climate hostile to or oblivious of God and literate only about space-time relativities.

As is well known, each of the recent Urbana (Illinois) Inter-Varsity conferences has gathered some eighteen thousand evangelical collegians. As many as half the participants in one conference attested that they had ventured a Christian commitment within the three preceding years. In due course this tide of evangelical students has swelled enrollments at conservative seminaries, and mainline denominations, faced by declining missionary volunteers, have looked increasingly to the interdenominational student movement for recruits.

To be sure, the evangelical resurgence reflected for some perhaps little more than a semipopular interest in ideas. The electronic church was led in large part by charismatic personalities more gifted in inspirational than in theological and apologetic concerns. Religious booksellers capitalized on the conservative advance by promoting bestseller works dwelling on personal experience, doctrinal controversy, eschatological speculation and the like. Evangelists established universities as rivals to secular institutions.

The Christian day school movement zoomed into high gear, often depicting public schools as essentially godless and amoral, even as champions of public schools often depicted private schools as elitist and racist. Newly formed evangelical universities often portrayed the secular campus as essentially atheistic and permissive in perspective. The severity of their judgment went far beyond that of long-established American evangelical colleges for whom the recovery of secular institutions for traditional theistic commitments remained an objective.

In such a climate of extremism, secular educators tended to dismiss the growing evangelical movement as an emotion-ridden aberration too intellectually impoverished to endure and regarded humanism as the firmly entrenched and quasi-official philosophy of the secular campus.

There are indications, however, that this verdict seriously misreads the facts. For one thing, the most recent Gallup poll indicates that spiritual interest on the part of university students has not run its course but remains a campus phenomenon. Four in five students consider religious beliefs important, two in five attend religious services weekly, one in three affirm that their religious commitments are deepening rather than weakening. While this religious inquiry takes a variety of turns—and includes an interest in cults such as Hare Krishna and the Unification Church as well as in

Islam and all branches of the Judeo-Christian movement—evangelical concerns still remain prominently at the center of the movement.

Meanwhile, more and more spokesmen from within the secular universities lament the decline of interest in the humanities and the attrition of educational core content that increasingly deprives students of a shared academic experience. They also fault the campuses for indifference to the persistent problems of philosophy, among them the reality of God and the objectivity of moral imperatives. As Stephen Muller, president of Johns Hopkins, puts it, the universities may be producing a generation of "highly skilled barbarians."

A further sign of continuing spiritual resurgence is the fact that in the presidential addresses of three recent leaders of the American Philosophical Association (APA), the subject of Christian theism was placed once again on the society's agenda. From within the APA has emerged a Society of Christian Philosophers which will soon publish a thought journal. In addition, the Institute for Advanced Christian Studies, together with Wm. B. Eerdmans Publishing Company, has begun the publication of "Studies in a Christian World View," a series of ten paperback texts at the junior college level. Written mostly by professors at Big Ten and other mainline universities, the series gives Christian perspective on various liberal arts disciplines. Evangelical texts are appearing also in philosophy and theology that underscore the importance of Christian theism for the intellectual as well as social life of the culture and that reach beyond empirical and historical methodology in probing ultimate reality. A growing confluence of literature by Jewish, Catholic, and Protestant scholars is now emerging as well; in a secular society whose pluralism lacks purpose and whose normless tolerance invites chaos, such literature is reaffirming the importance of biblical convictions and values. It was Nathan Pusey, former president of Harvard, who remarked at commencement exercises a generation ago that "the least that can be expected" from a university graduate is that he or she "pronounce the name of God without embarrassment."

MODERN LEARNING AT A CROSSROADS

Modern liberal learning is at a decisive crossroads. In accepting the Templeton Prize for Progress in Religion, Aleksandr Solzhenitsyn put the issue bluntly: "If I were asked today to formulate as concisely as possible the main cause of the ruinous Revolution that swallowed up some sixty million of our people," he said, "I could not put it more accurately than to repeat: 'Men have forgotten God; that's why all this has happened.' " This forsaking of God Solzhenitsyn proceeded to identify as "the principal trait of the entire twentieth century. . . . The entire twentieth century is being sucked into the vortex of atheism and self-destruction." It is one thing, he observed, that millions of human beings "have been corrupted and spiritually devastated by an officially imposed atheism"; it is another, hardly less disconcerting, that "the tide of secularism . . . has progressively inundated the West" so that "the concepts of good and evil have been ridiculed." It "has become embarrassing to appeal to eternal concepts, embarrassing to state that evil makes its home in the individual human heart before it enters a political system," Solzhenitsyn remarked; "the meaning of life in the West has ceased to be seen as anything more lofty than the 'pursuit of happiness.' "

Judgment for this eclipse of spiritual realities and for preoccupation with the space-time problematics of nature must fall more severely on us educators than upon our students. Indeed, students now often excel their professors in probing the transcendent world. Whether this interest will be permanently shunted to the edge of the classroom is simply another way of asking whether the world of liberal learning is willing to restore academic visibility once again to the priority of God and to ethical imperatives.

At a meeting of the American Association of University Professors shortly after Watergate, some members proposed a resolution condemning the political amorality that precipitated the national scandal. The proposal was quickly withdrawn, however, when someone observed that all major Watergate personalities had attended universities whose faculties are affiliated with A.A.U.P.

If the role of professors does not extend beyond social criticism to involve perpetual vigilance in grappling with and clarifying influential ideas and ideals, are we not accountable, at least in part, for a nation's loss of integrity and moral cohesion?

Is man but a physically upright and mentally clever animal or does he bear the image, however tarnished, of a holy and merciful personal Creator? Are we but complex creatures evolved from matter on an inconsequential planet itself the product of an unconscious collision of blind forces, or is the universe the work of a solicitous Creator who summons us to entrust our well-being and destiny to him? Does human existence move only toward cessation of life or are there, in fact, transcendent finalities and ultimate destinies in the offing? Contemporary education seems to escape, if not to evade, such issues and in so doing shortchanges learning by trivializing truth and the good.

While the verdict that intellectuals give on God and the good may not decide the ultimate destiny of contemporary culture, that verdict will nonetheless judge their competence as intellectual and moral analysts to whom are entrusted the fortunes of oncoming generations. When the Roman Empire collapsed in ignominious ruin, it was not the nobles and sages who perpetuated the moral fortunes of the West but rather the scattered people of God who lived according to spiritual and ethical imperatives.

What may well be at stake in the crisis of modern learning is not simply the significant survival of society but especially the significant survival of the university. Academia must recover the conviction and promulgation of shared values, of which in the West that of God has been supreme. Unless it does so, the fading space-time relativities will by default replace what was once the vision of God and of the good, and will doom man to mistake himself and his neighbor for passing shadows in the night, transient oddities with no future but the grave.

The Evangel and
Public Duty

*N*othing is more conspicuous in the American religious scene than the reentry of evangelical Christians into public affairs and their renewed interest in long-neglected cultural concerns. A long-smoldering uneasy conscience over sociopolitical detachment during the last generation has gradually escalated into aggressive political engagement accelerated by the last election campaign and extended by the electronic church, particularly through the activities of Moral Majority, Religious Roundtable, and related movements on the religious right.

Evangelical political activism imported a sense of evangelistic urgency into the political arena. But it lacked an articulate covering philosophy of political involvement and a comprehensively coordinated strategy. For one thing, the ecumenical political left, with its lingering social gospel enthusiasms, collapsed more quickly than expected. For another, the style of evangelical public involvement had been protest more than theory. This left the effort vulnerable to ambiguity in bridging from biblical imperatives to

This essay first appeared in the Spring-Summer 1982 issue of the Christian Legal Society Quarterly.

specific political commitments and even to conflicting and rival priorities.

There is no reason to think that evangelicals will form a distinctive political party with a detailed program of legislative objectives. Despite their appeal to an authoritative Bible, evangelicals disagree over baptism, glossolalia, and eschatology. It would be unrealistic to think that on nondoctrinal matters they will differ any less. Yet despite their diversity, evangelicals have in the past shaped spectacular alliances for evangelism and world missions. And in theological matters as well, their commonalities far outweigh their divergences from each other. An evangelical coalition on political and social issues could have a decisive impact on public morality and political perspectives.

Some attention to political philosophy, objectives, and strategy could spare the movement considerable internal grief and public misperception. Candid dialogue on the evangel and public affairs may help clarify perspectives for fellow evangelicals who seek evangelical fulfillment of both the church's world task of evangelism and of public duty.

Some evangelical leaders have already institutionalized their special concerns into competitive movements, whether on the left, on the right, or somewhere between or above both. Some wonder whether evangelicals should use the categorial distinctions of secular politics of the right or left instead of orienting their views only to biblical referents; others see this as a way of befuddling irreducible distinctions. Some of these movements (on the right, left, or middle) also have their own intramural struggles. Subtle differences on particular issues sometimes become a basis for rather sharp divisions.

The secular media not infrequently publicize and exploit these conflicts. Many secular reporters of our permissive society are not fully at home, moreover, in a discussion of moral absolutes and write from a stance that sees fascist overtones in evangelical concerns. And ecumenical spokespersons have misrepresented the evangelical political thrust as a breach of church-state separation. This despite ecumenism's own long involvement in much the same way, although predominantly on the left rather than on the right.

For these reasons, and also for the sake of authentic evangelical engagement, evangelicals must imperatively assess where they stand in respect to political involvement. We must ask whether we are ensconced as we ought to be and whether in the realm of public affairs we truly know where we are going, or where we ought to be going, and why.

SOME PERSPECTIVES FOR STUDY AND DISCUSSION

Let me project some personal perspectives that may stimulate study and discussion.

The Existence of Moral Absolutes

Moral absolutes exist. They are not simply of private relevance but hold decisive public importance as well. As a nation, America is fully answerable to ethical ultimates both in personal life and in national commitments. No society that disregards ethical finalities can long postpone ignominious collapse. Educators should therefore confront value clarification in the public schools where one person's values are frequently seen to be just as legitimate as another's and where a relativistic view of morality all too often prevails.

The Absence of Theocracy

Whereas in Old Testament times God's people lived in the divinely appointed context of the Hebrew theocracy, Christians today are dispersed worldwide as a new regenerate society and live amid a variety of political contexts, none of them a theocracy. Talk of the status of America as a Christian nation should not imply that the United States is a covenant nation standing in the same theocratic relationships to God as did the ancient Jewish state.

The Ultimate Ground for Law and Morality

The sovereign God is known by devout Jews and Christians to be the source, stipulator, and sanction of the right and the good. He is the ultimate ground of law and morality. He defines human rights and responsibilities and the powers and limits of human institutions. In matters of law and morality there is therefore a higher referent than the will of the state or the will of the majority, namely, the will of God.

This emphasis runs counter to modern theories of jurisprudence. John Rawl's standard text on *A Theory of Justice* (Belknap Press, 1971)—in which he champions enforced redistribution of wealth, for example—has no index reference to religion, Christianity, Christ, Bible, revelation, or sin. The distinction between good and bad law has vanished from most modern discussions; debate focuses instead on the question whether law is constitutional or unconstitutional. In this contest the Supreme Court is considered the ultimate arbiter. But if there are no criteria other than the preferences or prejudices of the justices, not even the Supreme Court can distinguish law as intrinsically good or bad. The Constitution, moreover, does not cover such issues as abortion and sexual privacy (homosexuality) or racial and sexual "equality of outcomes" (economic redistribution; affirmative action). In the absense of absolutes, can an alternative to relativism on these and other issues be justified?

Motivations for Advancing Justice

Christians have highly specific motivations for advancing justice: God's creation of humankind in the divine image and the universal call to repentance and redemption, and God's published imperative of universal justice all confer a special dignity upon human life.

Knowing God's Will

Scripture "thoroughly equips" the people of God "for every good work" (2 Timothy 3:17). The Christian priority is the need to know the revealed will of God which, along with other biblically given imperatives, includes the divinely stipulated principles of social ethics.

Civil Government's Role

God wills civil government as an institution for preserving justice and promoting peace and order in fallen society. While the

Bible prescribes no single form of government, it does repudiate some forms of political existence (e.g., state absolutism and social anarchy).

All human beings are duty bound to advance justice and to protest injustice. Whether others do so or not, Christians should identify themselves with the whole body of humanity and speak up in the name of transcendent right and justice. They should do so not simply when Christians suffer discrimination or oppression but also when any people so suffer. Christians and non-Christians alike have the same right to seek and the same duty to promote justice throughout the political order.

The Christian must expound the divinely disclosed purposes for which God ordains civil government. Christians must exemplify justice in social relationships, must challenge protracted injustice, and must be ready to suffer legal penalties rather than engage in revolutionary hostility if conscience requires public disobedience of the authorities.

The Importance of Religious Freedom

The primary flash point of a Christian political witness is religious liberty. Christians should be perceived in public affairs not merely as proponents of their own rights, but first of all as spokespersons for universal human dignity and rights under God, for disputing the pretensions of tyrannical rulers to absolute sovereignty over human life, and for promoting as the highest priority for all persons the individual's right to appeal to God's will and to a good conscience. Christians should champion and preserve constitutional guarantees of religious freedom for all persons as a fundamental human and civic right.

This basic commitment best meets secular complaints that the evangelical promotion of moral imperatives in national life poses a sectarian threat to democratic rights. Christian engagement in public affairs instead involves defending the right to dissent on the ground of conscience.

Freedom to appeal to the known will of God above Caesar's dictates preserves citizens from arbitrary political compulsion to do what God opposes and what contravenes conscience. Repression of religious freedom not only soon strips away the possibility of openly preaching the gospel but it otherwise also impedes voluntary fulfillment of the will of God in society. Christians should support legislation that includes individual freedom to persuade others voluntarily to recognize the transcendent nature of justice.

Civil Government's Limitations and the Church's Distinctive Mission

Civil government has an important but limited role in earthly affairs; it is not omnicompetent. Through the church God wills certain purposes and objectives in fallen history. The church is his appointed instrumentality for advancing the gospel and the ministry of grace in a call for voluntary commitment. Other purposes and objectives he achieves through civil government as a designated instrumentality for coercively preserving justice and restraining disorder. The Bible affords the church no basis for promoting evangelistic objectives by political means and affords the state no basis for promoting political objectives by ecclesiastical means. The notion that either the state or the church can achieve social utopia (the kingdom of God) on earth, as romanced by the social gospel, overlooks the fact of human sinfulness. Human perfectibility awaits the *eschaton*. This fact attests both the limitations of civil government and the church's distinctive mission in society.

Responsible Stewardship

As "owner of the universe" (Aquinas) God stipulates how creatures are to act in relation to the animate and inanimate worlds, toward each other, and toward him. On the basis of creation he mandates monogamous marriage and productive work, constitutes every person in some respects his or her brother's/sister's/neighbor's keeper, and approves private property as a responsible stewardship. The divine affirmation of capital punishment for murder (Genesis 9:6) also precedes the giving of the Decalogue.

The Right to Life

The present generation's most horrendous injustice lies in its wanton destruction of prenatal human life, an action by which our society shows brazen disrespect for the dignity and worth of the human fetus. The deliberate medical extinction of a million human fetuses a year exceeds the appalling evil of infanticide in pre-Christian paganism and approves a practice that civilizational conscience in all earlier decades considered reprehensible and morally vicious. It is supremely ironic that a society that declares human rights an absolute priority should retract the right to life of fetal life it engenders. "No plague, no war has so devastated the land."[1]

When childbirth would endanger the mother's life abortion can be morally justifiable. The fetus seems less than human, moreover, in cases of extreme deformity in which rational and moral capacities integral to the *imago Dei* are clearly lacking. The scriptural correlation of sexual intercourse with marriage and the family, furthermore, implies an ethical basis for voluntary abortion in cases of incest and rape. But the ready sacrifice of fetal life as a means of sexual gratification and of birth control is monstrous.

Abortion on demand has become an earthshock to the structures of marriage and the family. It restructures the role and duty of parents, it undermines the virtues of motherhood, and it accommodates a breakdown of conscience that can readily dispense also with the elderly once they become senile and, like fetuses in their weak and helpless condition, cannot protect and maintain themselves.

The Sanctity of Family Life

The sanctity of family life as a decisive biblical concern raises a whole cluster of logically related contemporary issues including adultery, divorce, prostitution, and the lax media handling of moral permissiveness and casual sex. All of these bear in one way or another on the validity of the monogomous family as the basic unit of society. Contrary to the tendency of a morally profligate social order to resist laws against adultery as a remnant of Victorian prudery, adulterous relationships should be condemned as ultimately destructive of the social order and considered legal ground for divorce. The debate over the human or civil rights of homosexuals should not be confused by analogies with race discrimination or concerns of religious freedom; people are born black or white or brown but they are not born gay. Gays can and ought to alter their lifestyle even if we must not infringe upon their political rights.

The Duty to Work

The duty to work precedes the fall of humankind and is grounded in God's assigning to Adam, on the basis of creation, the task of keeping and dressing the garden. Humanity's work is to shape the cosmos in conformity to the moral and spiritual purposes of the Creator. It is to be constructive, not destructive, and hence is to glorify God and promote the good of humankind.

Not the biblical view of work but the misconception of work as a divine penalty, an evil to be avoided, underlies this comment in a national newsmagazine: "When God foreclosed on Eden, he condemned Adam and Eve to go to work. From the beginning, the Lord's word said that work was something bad: a punishment, the great stone of mortality and toil laid upon a human spirit that might otherwise soar in the infinite, weightless playfulness of grace."[2] But a person without work loses his sense of worth and dignity.

The duty of work implies the right to work. The New Testament correlation of working and eating ("If a man will not work, he shall not eat" [2 Thessalonians 3:10]) implies that a society in which joblessness prevails should consider the provision of constructive work a prime concern.

Concern for the Poor

Response to the plight of the destitute is a prime test of social sensitivity. The God of the Bible has an "eye for the poor" and each person is "his brother's keeper." Concern for the destitute is a universal imperative, one that imposes duties upon all human beings; it devolves not only upon Free World countries but upon all countries, including the Soviet bloc and dollar-laden OPEC nations. The Christian is to respond promptly to the needs of the "household of faith" and of his or her "neighbor"—that is, those at one's side who are in want—and also to both the emergency needs and standing plight of the impoverished who cannot help themselves. He is bidden to do so, moreover, "in Christ's name."

General Revelation as Basis for Judgment

Unlike the Hebrew theocracy, which stood in a special covenantal relationship to Yahweh, the pluralistic nations are judged by the light of general revelation universally available on the basis of God's creation of humankind. Amos's indictment of ancient Israel's six pagan neighbor nations is particularly instructive. Damascus is doomed for threshing Gilead "with sledges having iron teeth" (1:3); Gaza for taking "captive whole communities" and delivering them to Edom (1:6); Tyre for delivering up a whole people to Edom and for forgetting "a treaty of brotherhood" (1:9). Edom is doomed for pursuit with the sword and for "stifling all compassion" (1:11); Ammon for ripping open the pregnant women of Gilead "in order to extend his borders" (1:13); Moab for burning to lime the bones of the king of Edom (2:1). These indictments for national crimes include havoc wrought by invasion, occupation, and captivity; by bartering slaves and captives of war as a matter of trade; by atrocity and treachery and other social evils.

These specifics emerge from the history of these heathen nations in international affairs. The clear assumption is that ravishing neighbor nations, selling slaves and prisoners of war, and violating treaties are all infractions known to be unjust independently of the theocratic revelation to Israel. God discloses himself to all nations in his judgments (cf. Isaiah 13-24; Jeremiah 25:12-14; Ezekiel 32:1-32; Amos 9:1-4; Nahum 1-3).

Peacemaking in a Nuclear Age

This representative agenda of international atrocities that spites God's ordination of civil government to promote peace focuses modern interest on the massive and continuing nuclear arms buildup in a technological age capable of destroying not only humankind but the cosmos. In 1980 the Soviet Union alone spent $175 billion and the United States $115 billion for defense purposes; lesser powers budgeted additional billions. Continuing production of deadly atomic missiles capable of destroying vast populations and inflicting incalculable ecological damage challenges all modern nations to fulfill their peacekeeping role and to boldly condemn aggression by all predator powers.

In face of the astronomical military budgets of the super-powers, Christians must maintain a strong and sustained witness to Christ, the prince of peace and King of kings; must pray urgently for peace among the nations; must press upon these powers an awareness of the damage done by the arms race to each other and to themselves; and must deplore the self-condemning track record of predator powers whose expansionist policies provoke ever-escalating expenditures that might ideally be deployed to more constructive social uses.

Some Christians believe that war is always immoral. Others believe that nuclear missiles involve a quantum leap of destructive power that outmodes just war. Still others believe that massive twentieth century totalitarian aggression and the murder of multitudes of civilians by Nazis, Stalinists, and Maoists itself constitutes a quantum leap of tyrannical disregard for human life and property, and that not to challenge it is immoral and a matter of Christian lovelessness.

The Christian Community as a New Society

Christians are in a weak position before God and before the world if they condone in their own ranks injustices that they deplore in society at large. Someone has said that no one is in more danger in the Bible than the self-righteous.

The Christian community is a new society that lives out its two-world citizenship by the resurrection power of its living Lord and by the dynamic of the Holy Spirit. If the church is to have institutional integrity and moral force in a political witness to the secular world, it must display a distinctive Christian lifestyle and deathstyle. That lifestyle must reflect the church's deep moral convictions on such fundamental concerns of social ethics as marriage and divorce, work, abortion, homosexuality, war and peace, property rights and other human rights. If religious and moral commitments are a basis of community action, no body of community is in a better position to demonstrate the implications than is the believing church in her own social life.

The early church did not endeavor to impose Christian morality on the unbelieving world but called believers to live by biblical principles: "I have written you . . . not to associate with sexually immoral people—not at all meaning the people of this world who are immoral. . . . In that case you would have to leave this world. But now I am writing you that you must not associate with anyone who calls himself a brother but is sexually immoral . . ." (1 Corinthians 5:9-11; cf. 6:9-20). Instead of seeking to impose theocratic patterns upon society in general, the church is to be a christocracy over which Christ rules by the Scriptures.

The Moral Conscience of Humankind

Pluralistic states, we said, are judged on the basis of universal divine revelation, while the Hebrew theocracy was accountable also for obedience to Yahweh's specific commands given by special revelation. Judeo-Christian religion rests upon a particular revelation rooted in a special religious history. Yet its message is in certain respects universal and, in fact, fundamentally so.

The psalmist has the pagan nations in view when he writes:

O LORD, the God who avenges,
  O God who avenges, shine forth.
Rise up, O Judge of the earth;
  pay back to the proud what they deserve.
  . . . .

They slay the widow and the alien;
  they murder the fatherless.
  . . . .

They band together against the righteous
  and condemn the innocent to death.
                                    (Psalm 94:1-2, 6, 21)

Yahweh judged Israel's neighbor nations not because they had violated the myriad of specific laws he had given the Hebrews, but because of violent oppression and human victimization that were universally wrong (cf. Revelation 18, where Babylon is judged as a type of the nations).

Just as Judaism connects the ethics of Sinai with the ethics of creation, so Christianity relates the ethics of the Sermon on the Mount as well as of Sinai with that of creation. The apostle Paul was fully aware that the Roman state was not a "Christian government." Yet in Romans 13:9 he adduces the prohibition of adultery, murder, covetousness, and stealing on the apparent premise that the second table of the Decalogue—that is, the social aspect of the law—is somehow anticipated by the conscience of all persons as part of the created givenness of humanity. These precepts speak of the inviolability of human life, of preservation of the integrity of family life, and of property rights—principles that today are under aggressive attack. And as Paul notes earlier in this same letter (2:14-15), even the Gentiles at times attest both in conscience and in outward behavior an awareness of certain moral imperatives that were clarified, reinforced, and supplemented to the Jews by the Sinai revelation. Some cognitive awareness independent of special historical revelation is stamped upon the moral consciousness of humankind on the basis of divine creation. The spiritual and ethical rebellion of the Gentiles occurs, therefore, in a context of an inner responsible knowledge of the living God as the source of moral law and as the stipulator of the good (1:32).

It may be that Paul viewed the social commandments of the Mosaic law as specifying a person's duty on the basis of the universal law of love for neighbor as an obligation already known by creation and first violated by Cain (Genesis 4:9). At any rate, for Paul the claim of love—since it fulfills God's will—is superior even to the claim of the ruler.[3] Love carries out at one and the same time not only God's just purposes for the state but also God's will for the individual in social relations. Love is outwardly expressed by observing God's commandments governing human relationships. But love also discharges Christian duty to the state, since it fulfills the whole law both by embracing the commandments externally and by observing them inwardly in terms of spiritual motivation. For that reason Paul adds to the specific social commandments of the Decalogue the rider "and whatever other commandment there may be" (13:9). The Christian need fear the power of the state and its sword only when he or she acts contrary to the very ends God has set before the state (13:4-7). To live in neighbor-love is to inwardly cherish the social commandments of the law and to outwardly advance the ends God has in view for civil government.

The Supposed Irrelevance of Moral Absolutes

The notion that a political democracy requires ethical pluralism and unqualified tolerance of moral diversity implies an irrelevance of moral absolutes that can lead only to social chaos. Now often coordinated with this sorry premise is the equally fallacious assumption that moral absolutes in public life are of special concern only to totalitarian and dictatorial nations. Totalitarian government, even if it does pretentiously and arbitrarily consider itself the source of all moral distinctions, does indeed frequently stamp out vices that the democracies do not even challenge. But to suspend the content of acceptable morality only upon individual preference or upon cultural consensus is to succumb to relativity in ethics and, in turn, to civilizational chaos.

When individuals and nations spurn God's transcendent law, they place themselves over against the divinely ordained course of history that the Creator of all worlds and peoples, the One to whom all nations are answerable, has ordained. In the Bible the nations stand from the beginning in responsible moral relationships to God. Law has a religious basis and sanction; it is grounded in divinely willed justice for which people and nations are universally accountable. The purpose of statute law is to redirect fallen humankind's civil propensities so that justice prevails in community life. Statute law particularizes the content of justice and love in social relationships. Community tolerance need not imply moral permissiveness. God dooms political entities whose immorality becomes intolerable to him; the vices of both tiny Sodom and Gomorrah and of mighty Rome invited their own destruction. The social commandments of the Decalogue reappear in the Book of Revelation as criteria relevant to the judgment of all people and nations.

The Legislation of Values

The question of whether civil government should legislate values and, if so, which values should be imposed and enforced and on what grounds is crucially urgent. It is clear that in some instances, notably in the case of Prohibition, the federal government has legislated specific morals; some say that morality is precisely what legislation is aimed to govern. The religious right has protested what it considers a federal legislation of immorality, notably the funding of abortions, which involves using tax dollars to help others commit a wrong whose consequences for the fetus are irreversible.

The view of libertarians is that the state should concern itself with moral behavior only when it involves a nonconsenting third party. The special concern of politics, they say, is with legality and not with morality. For libertarianism, legislation defines the public duty of all citizens, not bureaucratically imposed beliefs about ethics. While such legislation may be morally substantive or promote moral ends, it does not seek moral virtue but simply legal conformity. Such legislation, moreover, is concerned not with inner spiritual attitudes and moral motivation but simply with outward conformity to law. Neither Christians nor humanists, say the libertarians, are to promote metaphysical or moral beliefs by coercive enforcement. In short, the special providence of civil government is with what is legal. The state is not to elaborate nor to implement what is ethical; government's proper concern is legality not morality. Sin is indeed wicked, but the question of sin per se is not proper to civil government; only the question of sin's related legality or illegality is a concern of civil power.

Libertarians emphasize that my freedom to swing my fist ends only where the tip of another's nose begins. But no sooner is the thesis stated than problems appear.

Shall we decriminalize marijuana for personal use? One might say "yes, but restrict the amount one may possess and the place of such use."

But do we really have a right to protect people from harming themselves? One might suggest that a minor should be so protected since a minor has no freedom until he or she is sixteen or eighteen years old. We require minors to attend school until age sixteen for their own good even if their parents or the children don't approve. The state can properly make such decisions affecting those below a certain age, it might be replied, but such intervention is improper after one reaches sixteen.

But are legal modifications of behavior proper after one reaches sixteen? Shall we or shall we not decriminalize marijuana for use by consenting adults? Is not the private use of marijuana wholly a personal decision?

Yet some conservatives who promote this view of freedom would regulate chemical additives and preservatives in food products (e.g., the addition of nitrate to bacon or hot dogs) while others would oppose such legislation on the ground that none need buy these products. Californians who wanted "the law off our backs" by insisting that government should not mandate sex education courses in public schools also wanted laws requiring doctors to report to authorities the names of teenage girls for whom they prescribe birth control pills.

The point is that, despite the desirable emphasis on liberty, both sides selectively decide just what restrictions to impose or ban and often make private or special interest rather than cognitive consistency the deciding factor. Some citizens want to rid television of crime, sex, and violence because they induce aggressiveness, at least subconsciously. Others oppose children's commercials because youngsters are specially vulnerable to commercial exploitation. And some object to child evangelism on the ground that only consenting adults are mature enough to make responsible religious commitments.

Yet parents are not required to make their children available for child evangelism and children are not required to listen to television.

Apart from the fact that those who promote public restriction of behavior apply that rule selectively, we must admit that the line between my rights and someone else's is not always clear. When I swing my fist wildly it is not always self-evident that another's nose begins where I think it does.

Social democracy usually assumes that I am "my brother's keeper," and modern welfare philosophy rests on the assumption that we have a duty to help. What does this imply for those who are unwell and who cannot help even themselves? To what extent do I have a duty to help another if I have no duty to keep him from hurting society if not from hurting himself? People who destroy themselves usually expect others to pick up the pieces. In view of the rising cost of public health and social services, do we have a right to regulate what undermines others (e.g., drug abuse, alcohol addiction, cigarette smoking)? A frequent reply is that we must indeed help others but in doing so must not hurt them by depriving them of what they want. But the fact is that while profligacy in use of natural resources or pollution of environment may not hurt any one person directly, such abuses may nonetheless hurt all of society indirectly. Do not rights imply also the legitimacy of at least some regulation? But where does another's nose begin? Should my rights extend far enough to do anything I choose just so long as I do not injure a second or third party?

Even those who would restrict human behavior disagree as to how and what. Some would restrict only behavior that hurts people directly, others would also restrict behavior that hurts people indirectly. Prostitution, some say, is a victimless crime—a matter of social pleasure. But what of the young girls that are exploited, even if they willingly sell their bodies? And what about adulterous relationships—should they be considered unlawful? Or should laws against adultery be considered illegal and be repudiated as a vestige of an outmoded Puritan code? Should adultery be considered not illegal per se but nonetheless as legal grounds for divorce?

If we completely isolate the political arena from moral absolutes we inevitably condemn it to political relativism. Unless libertarian ethics is infused with some specific content beyond merely saying that my rights end where yours begin, then the principles can be applied in many and conflicting ways. The person who says that public moral concerns boil down to a matter of personal choice or to the individual liberty of consenting adults, may be intending merely to approve abortion and homosexuality but cannot easily avoid sanctioning such items as drug trafficking and euthanasia as well. Almost all legislative issues end up involving a moral choice. All legislation reflects a moral judgment and impinges on conduct.

Selecting Moral Guidelines

Over and above affirming the legitimacy of civil government for the stipulated objectives of preserving peace and order, the Bible, on the basis of a divine-command morality, sets forth certain enduringly valid social principles. It does not, however, set forth the detailed particularities of statute law for pluralistic governments as it did for the Old Testament theocracy. In a pluralistic society legislation is not based on theocratically and bureaucratically imposed spiritual and ethical beliefs championed as the public duty of all citizens by one of several community components.

On Mount Sinai, God legislated certain absolutes for the Hebrew nation. When in heated debate in the U.S. Senate, Senator Jesse Helms referred to "the set of instructions that came down from Mount Sinai." Senator Lowell Weicker replied, "We are not running this country by divine commandment or instructions from Mount Sinai." Senator Weicker's reply leaves untouched the question whether the Sinai imperatives nonetheless retain relevance for all the nations and if so on what basis. Even if compromise is the nature of politics in a fallen world and approximations of justice are vulnerable to continuing refinement, what objective guidelines are relevant to the political articulation of justice?

The libertarian view is formally valuable, but it leaves open the question of the ideal content of legislation. Amid the growing emphasis today on recovering a fundamental morality the question remains largely unresolved as to what values society should impose. There is considerable renewed discussion about ethical guidelines, yet in much of this talk the realm of moral absolutes remains out of view. Even the call for principles formulation by the courts, rather than mere ad hoc judicial judgment in specific cases, does not in and of itself identify a substantive or normative content. Two influential books on political philosophy, Robert Nozick's *Anarchy, State and Utopia* (1974) and John Rawl's *A Theory of Justice* (1971), for example, reach divergent views on the morality of enforced economic distribution. Congresspersons and justices have repeatedly slipped their own preferred values into the positions they espouse. Even the life-tenured Supreme Court justices hold somewhat divergent values; sometimes the majority judgment has diverged from the values of the past or from those of a majority of citizens in the present. What moral guidelines are available to public institutions concerning matters of empirical uncertainty?

Moral Justification in a Pluralistic Society

The religious right evoked a storm of secular reaction when some of its leaders emphasized that America is a Christian country where most citizens still believe in Christian values and urged that the nation's Christian foundations be restored by political renewal. A good government, it was said, will uphold the moral principles stipulated by the Bible. Christian standards, rather than the permissive alternatives preferred by a secular society, should therefore be championed as legislative ideals. Christians consider the social imperatives of Scripture—protection of monogamous marriage and property rights, respect for the dignity of human life, capital punishment for murder, and so on—important for national well-being and survival. Either explicitly or implicitly the Bible declares what the truly just state will legislate as right and good in public life.

A number of ecumenical critics hurriedly lampooned the Moral Majority for thrusting a biblically based religious ethic upon a pluralistic democracy. Spokespersons on the political left raised the specter of a religious establishment that might dominate the state, although lobbyists for the National Council of Churches had themselves earlier and often advocated specific legislative positions on the ground of their supposed religio-ethical superiority, even if the biblical basis for such ecumenically affirmed positions was often obscure. Moreover, the federal government's possible encroachment on religious conscience in respect to positions on abortion and homosexuality, for example, had now also become an issue.

To say that the Bible stipulates what government ideally legislates inevitably evokes political debate among rival religious and philosophical traditions, a conflict that is properly no concern of government. Only a totalitarian society, whether theocratic or atheistic, imposes metaphysical beliefs upon its citizens. The Bible nowhere stipulates statute laws that pluralistic governments are to impose in the name of a divine-command morality. No nation today stands in a theocratic covenantal relationship with the God of all nations. The Bible nowhere adduces statute law to be theocratically imposed upon the pluralistic powers of the world on the ground of God's specially revealed word and command. The metaphysical grounds on which citizens affirm the content of justice is of high theological, philosophical, and apologetic importance but it is not a matter of political interest. The state can take sides in matters of religious or metaphysical disputation only by disregarding religious freedom. To be sure, unless a methodology for validating transcendent values exists, moral alternatives have no persuasive epistemological basis. But adjudicating between religions and philosophies is not the task of civil government; such concerns fall outside the scope of political authority.

Metaphysical assumptions underlie not only Christian but also non-Christian ethical positions. The humanist is self-consciously committed to naturalism, and process-philosophy's emphasis on ecological concerns is not unrelated to its undergirding conviction that nature is streaked with divinity. But the religious or metaphysical foundations of values are not of governmental relevance. It is wrong for the Christian or the humanist or for anyone else to try to impose a theological or metaphysical morality as such upon a pluralistic society. Religious freedom is an indispensable treasure that must not be jeopardized in the public debate over values. Moral justification in the public order must be civil rather than theological, even though the civil is privately informed by the theological. Civil government defines what is unlawful, not what is sinful.

Moral Majority's tardy insistence that their movement is not a religious effort based on theological considerations is propitious, even if they have drawn fire for appealing to "pluralistic" rather than to "Christian" supports for their public positions. The use of political means to enforce sectarian principles in a pluralistic society has no biblical legitimacy and is incompatible with church-state separation.

Promiscuous relativists who banner the slogan "do your own thing" are not alone in resisting evangelical political morality and other public morality. They are joined by others with social and public concerns who, while saying "don't push your preferred ethical positions on me," would like to push their preferred alternatives on us. Surely the Christian will remain centrally concerned with legitimate warrants for evangelical social positions no less than reflective non-Christians will probe warrants for their specific proposals. But how in a pluralistic arena does a sectarian view of ethics—whether theistic, humanistic, or whatever else—ideally relate to a general view of public justice and the good? What is an adequate rationale for espousing specific legislative options in a pluralistic society?

Some Proposed Bases for Legislated Morality

1. The appeal to tradition. Human beings are prone to opt for the values they have inherited, that is, for tradition. The appeal to tradition as a basis for community morality is common to many lands. In the United States it is reflected by the slogan, "The American way." Many countries that welcome Western scientific and technological learning seek to offset its moral vacuums and sensate character by emphasizing national, cultural, and religious heritage. The appeal to inherited values thus gains an aura of patriotism, cultural inheritance, and historical consensus.

Shall we revert to tradition to decide our values and legislative imperatives? One virtue of constitutional law is that it provides a relatively objective standard for judging successive regimes. But does the Constitution protect only those values that coincide with traditional interests? Does an unambiguous American tradition exist, for example, on discrimination against minorities? Tradition can be adduced on many sides of an issue and mean many things; it can be invoked both to accredit and to discredit causes. What often underlies the appeal to tradition is a selective invocation of some one preferred tradition from among many traditions. Even then, this preferred tradition can be interpreted tendentiously, as when Jesus is declared a socialist or a pacifist. If mere tradition is invoked, moreover, can there be progress beyond the past? And how does one judge between rival traditions in one country's traditions and another's? In a passing reference whose significance he does not pursue, John Hart Ely asks: "Is . . . Jesus Christ [part of the American tradition]? It's hard to see why not."[4]

The possibility becomes obvious, then, of discriminating between traditions, of reaffirming The Great Tradition among the lesser traditions, and of witnessing to the biblical heritage which as an inspired tradition has shaped many aspects of Western culture. Not even when the debate over preferred alternatives is stated solely in terms of tradition can the secular mind show the superiority of other traditions over that of the Judeo-Christian view which carries discussion of the good and the lawful back to God the creator of human beings. Different countries have different cultural mixes, and in some where Christian convictions are or have been deeply written into the consciousness of the masses, an appeal to Christian tradition may be fully appropriate in the public arena. Such an appeal is appropriate as long as it does not encourage a misimpression that tradition is self-justifying and does not dissolve the logos of law into the prevailing ethos.

2. *The appeal to natural law.* Another appeal advanced to promote the legislation of morality is that to natural law, which is said to be stamped upon universal human nature. Unlike an appeal either to special revelation or to national or cultural tradition, that to innate standards holds that human beings share common ethical norms able to guarantee the well-being of society.

The difficulty with natural law theory is that moral philosophers who champion it do not agree among themselves as to the moral principles that it supposedly validates. No universally shared system of morality has, in fact, survived the fall of humankind.

To be sure, one need not succumb to the claims of positivistic or humanistic anthropologists who say that the ethical differences among human groups are so extensive and radical that the only remaining undisputed dictum is that a man should not venture sex relations with his mother. (Even this last rule is now being implicitly disputed by those social scientists who claim that incest may have therapeutic values.) What happens is that anthropologists too easily interpret instances of moral degeneracy as being entrenched moral norms. What is recognized as morally evil is more widespread than is sometimes implied, even if no universally consistent corpus of ethical values prevails.

Every society recognizes that the distinction between good and evil is a genuine one. Yet not even the conviction that all people are created equal is self-evident. The American Constitution as a frame of government makes no reference to natural law. And it is not demanded by the Pauline reference to "the law written upon the hearts" even of Gentiles who lacked special revelation but who nonetheless are related to universal divine revelation (Romans 2:14-15).

Ely observes that "natural law has been summoned in support of all manner of causes in this country—some worthy, others nefarious—and often on both sides of the same issue."[5] It was used, for example, to support both sides of the slavery issue.

The supposed fixed content of natural law is either too general and abstract to provide specific guidance or too specific to be truly universal. It is, in short, too ambiguous to be helpful in the difficult questions of public policy.

Yet neither the lack of universally shared values nor the radical views of relativists requires a rejection of moral absolutes. As Ely says, "It is no fairer to cite the dissenting morality of Adolf Hitler to prove the nonexistence of moral truth than it would be to invoke the views of the Flat Earth Society to prove there is not a correct position on the shape of the earth."[6] Nor does the inadequacy of natural law as a ground for the content of legislation prove that no acceptable ground of common political action exists.

3. The appeal to social consensus. The content of legislation, which is not revelationally stipulated for pluralistic governments, may be suspended on a third option—social consensus or majority will. No life in community is possible without a widely shared consensus on what is lawful; statute law, it is said, should reflect the will of the majority.

Much of the current ferment in American society stems from the penetration of public institutions by humanist emphases. Evangelicals charge that public schools and universities, even political institutions, have become platforms for extending humanistic views and for implementing humanist objectives.

The Moral Majority and similar conservative political movements have called for counterefforts to resist the imposition of humanist objectives upon the citizenry at large and have tried to reverse legislation that they consider erosive of Christian values.

This conflict gained the semblance of an interreligious contest when it was emphasized that humanism is a naturalistic religion whose permissive views of abortion and homosexuality stand under biblical indictment. These factors bear significantly on church-state concerns in view of the one-sided promotion of humanist positions in public institutions. While majority rule may as readily reflect humanist, Christian, or some other majority, church-state separation precludes channeling the debate into a dispute merely over rival metaphysical options.

Moral Majority has clarified its stance by underplaying specific theological presuppositions and concentrating rather on the moral quality of legislation. While most of its supporters are devoted to biblical standards and insist that most American citizens are also, the organization's announced goals do not include imposing Christian morality as such upon non-Christians, but simply manifesting in legislation the public consensus that it purports to reflect. Values are to be legislated on the nonecclesiastical ground that they are most widely shared; the common morality or social consensus is to be translated into legal principles by connecting it with statute law.

Many observers argue, however, that a firm social consensus no longer exists; there are striking ambiguities of public conscience on many concerns. The political scene reflects a continuing struggle between conflicting groups concerning the definition of justice, one effectively dominated at present by temporary coalitions. Elected representatives are viewed as a reflection of this unsteady "consensus," one that on many issues discloses a mix of unresolved generalities and controversial specifics.

Is the appeal to a moral majority therefore antidemocratic? No more so, it would seem, and doubtless far less so, than if the positions of antimajority influences were to prevail. If a nondemocratic elite determines the laws of the land the pattern leads readily to the Soviet misconception of "democracy" in which people really have no voice in articulating the content of legislation.

The role of any majority is plain enough: While minorities can block legislation, majorities are in a better position to pass it. An ethically sensitive majority will, of course, be sensitive to minority rights. Yet minorities, Christian or non-Christian, will always face certain problems of conformity or nonconformity to majority consensus. Law is not coercive in that it allows noncompliance if one affirms the primacy of religious freedom; Christians know full well what it is to suffer penalties for noncompliance.

The weakness of the view that the majority will determine the content of legislation is that while it suspends on a majority vote the validity of the Christian or any other view of what is right, it provides no criterion for judging and assessing that consensus. A majority—even a majority of Americans—can be wrong. Majority rule is preferable to minority rule in that it provides a shelter against tyrants, but it does not of itself guarantee the rule of justice.

4. The appeal to the welfare of society. Some emphasize what they consider a higher principle than majority rule. The state's fundamental duty of preserving justice, they say, requires legislation that serves the public good. All legislation is to be justified by its social consequences, its contribution to the welfare of society.

But it is one thing to declare the good to be definitive of public justice and another to decide between competing definitions of the good. Augustine, Kant, Nietzsche, and Marx espouse very different views of how human beings ought to view and act toward each other. Champions of the welfare state define the welfare of humankind in Marxist terms. Others believe this approach to be a perversion; only a totalitarian government would presume to implement a system of laws designed to guarantee universal human welfare, an expectation, they say, that rests on a mistaken view of history and humankind.

In modern times emphasis on the public good has usually implied a utilitarian theory of ethics which identifies the content of human duty with what promotes "the good of the greatest number." But in recent decades this utilitarian emphasis on the majority good has been challenged on the ground that it ignores the good of the minority or of minorities—it compromises distributive justice. Moreover, since we cannot empirically anticipate all consequences of our actions, the approach is vulnerable to manipulation in the interest of divergent expectations.

The very notion that only its consequences constitute any act good and that no values or actions are intrinsically good in and of themselves runs counter to belief in antecedently fixed ethical principles. Moreover, no reason can be shown on utilitarian grounds why one ought to seek the greatest good of the greatest number. The concept is formally right that legislation ideally advances the public good. In establishing the content of good legislation, however, the formula does not carry us far beyond the emphasis merely on a public consensus which by its very nature will advance the concerns of the greatest number.

The apostle Paul does indeed insist that the ruler "is God's servant to do you good" (Romans 13:4); "rulers hold no terror for those who do right. . . . do what is right and he will commend you" (13:3). But Paul also holds that human beings are not completely out of touch with the good as specified by the will of God.

The Image of God and Public Morality

Although there is no universally shared system of absolutes, the Christian knows that God, who creates the state as an instrumentality for preserving justice, also preserves all human beings in accountable relationships to the good and right on the basis of general revelation. Moreover, the revealed moral principles of Scripture are not a sectarian ethic intended solely for Jews and Christians but are intended also for humankind universally.

On the basis of the created *imago Dei* every human person shares the divinely given forms of reason and of conscience that link humankind to the transcendentally good and just and holy God and to individual intimations of the divine ethical imperatives. However sullied it may be, the image of God in the human person is not totally eradicated by the fall. To be sure, the Bible alone gives the comprehensive content of divine ethics with propositional clarity. But remnants of God's moral claim nonetheless survive on the basis of the created *imago Dei* and supply an inner contact point between Christians and the secular community for bringing into relationship the good in the Christian revelational understanding and the general or public conception of the good.

The commitment to pluralistic government and to religious

pluralism implies that public morality can be determined apart from affirmation of a specific religious belief. Christian witness among modern nations therefore includes reinforcing God's claim upon the conscience and will of humankind universally in view of both God's creation of the human species in moral dignity and his endowment of human beings everywhere with inalienable rights.

The Christian and Legislative Action

This does not mean that a Christian citizenry must legally impose upon a secular society either the content of biblically revealed ethics or subscription to the truth of general divine revelation by which all people and nations will be and are presently being judged. The fact of God's universal endowment of human beings with inalienable rights is recognized and affirmed in the American charter political document, the Declaration of Independence.

While what ground one affirms for arriving at the morality of particular acts is of theological or philosophical importance and of great individual significance, one's theological or philosophical rationale is not the business of civil government. The state does not police and legislate the foundations of morality or the motivations of citizens for keeping the law. Its concern is with the content of legality and with outward conduct.

The Christian objective should not be to impose upon citizens a theology of revelation for understanding the content of social ethics. Rather Christians should support legislation that provides for all citizens the freedom to try to persuade others to recognize what is right and to do it, and to advance and support programs that coincide with what we believe a just society must champion.

There is one point, however, where the Christian in the political arena can properly declare God's revealed will and command to be a principle of political action, and that is where civil law requires him or her to do what contravenes what God requires, or requires him or her to do what God prohibits. In the political realm the Christian seeks by his or her actions to obey both God and governmental authorities. But when "the powers" require what violates God's command, the Christian like the apostles will openly declare his or her supreme allegiance: "We must obey God rather than men!" (Acts 5:29).

When Christian leaders are called upon for testimony before government agencies testing the climate of conviction on public issues, such spokesmen should be explicit about the supernatural warrants for Christian positions where such warrants exist. The apostle Paul did not hesitate to appeal to divine imperatives in testimony before Roman rulers. Christians oppose theft, murder, adultery, and abortion on demand because they live not by the law of the jungle but by the law of love. Compassionate concern for the weak and helpless is a biblical motif. The commandments of God define for Christians the content of the law of love. Christians also believe, as some non-Christians do, that these very norms of social ethics constitute a desirable moral tradition that should be perpetuated as elements of political justice, that these norms advance the public good, and that they are supremely worthy of the conscientious commendation of an ethically concerned majority.

There is another point in political engagement at which Christians may ideally, as an aspect of political involvement, publicly adduce biblical warrants for their legislative positions. Justice should, of course, be promoted by all human beings and not by Christians only. Christians should identify themselves openly with the body of humanity in a common concern to advance nondiscriminatory justice in public affairs. But after uniting in a common protest against political injustice, Christians are free to regroup in a distinctive public witness to the living God of justice and of justification, who makes known his holy will and law, who forgives sins and bestows new power to do the right. If Christians were to set the agenda for public protest against such evils or take a public initiative in advancing and supporting just laws as courses of action motivated by revelational concerns, they would spontaneously fix in the public mind the connection between those dedicated to biblically revealed norms and the promotion of ideal social order.

Proclaiming the Gospel

We are not enjoined to try to turn a twentieth-century state into a Christian government. But by its evangelistic task in society the church seeks to stimulate human beings voluntarily to recover the whole moral content of divine revelation and to inform humanity's conscience according to God's transcendent absolutes. While the theocratic stipulations of the Old Testament have no direct covenant significance for the United States or any other modern nation, the promises of divine blessing for individual obedience remain. As churches proclaim a gospel calling for personal decision they can legitimately also, as part of their evangelistic objective, attempt to win the nation for Christ. Such proclamation illumines both God's universal revelation on the basis of creation and his special redemptive revelation in the Bible. Here the general public "overhears" the Christian proclamation of the nature and ground of political duty rather than a direct political summons to secular society to bring itself under a divine-command morality. The church's mission to the mind and motives of nonbelievers is not a matter of ecclesiastical imposition but of voluntary inner persuasion of what is right.

The Christian knows that only in the light of scriptural controls can modern ethical perspectives escape relativism. The Christian knows that the God of creation has already stamped his claim on every human life. The Christian knows that the Decalogue gives the timelessly valid social ideals. The Christian knows that people and nations will be finally judged by the commandments of God. By evangelism he or she will commend these truths in the name of the God of justice and of justification.

But in the political arena he or she should commend ethical imperatives consistent with and reflective of the will of God on grounds that are familiar to the general public—that is, on the basis of the general good, of desirable facets of social consensus, and then of the best remnants of cultural heritage. If most citizens share a scripturally compatible view, then the Christian task force is indeed free to lead or stand with a moral majority. But the Christian must also defend and champion the civil rights even of those who live by offensive lifestyles. Freedom to sin is a necessary component of life in fallen society. Civil government does not define personal sin or seek to eliminate it; its concern is with the public good and with justice. The church preaches against lying; the state legislates not against lying per se but against misrepresentation in contracts or in consumer advertising or in guarantees.

Secular views of ethics, to be sure, cannot vindicate a final norm of the good or of justice. Even at a level of dialogue concerned only with the public good and social consequences, it is the biblically sanctioned alternative that best maintains itself; other approaches soon jeopardize the stability of community life and threaten public well-being. Secular justification of ethical decency is now so confused that the modern state tends increasingly to adduce its own foundations for civil order. Failure of the churches to inform Christian conscience, let alone public conscience, with a proper understanding of the purpose of civil government only abets this confusion. By its totalitarian rule the communist state provides an ideological interpretation that forcibly keeps the social consensus from falling into the kind of ethical relativism that increasingly overtakes democratic societies. The church has the urgent task of publicly proclaiming that only supreme loyalty to the will of God can withstand the dictatorial will of tyrants and the chaos that results in public affairs.

The role of government is not to stipulate absolutes but rather to protect statute laws that best preserve the imperative of justice in community life. Even if civil government now has no basis for legislating statute law on the ground that God reveals and commands it, it must nonetheless articulate what justice implies in social relationships. The state tries to express in legal particularities what conduct is most consistent with the moral absolutes that underlie law (e.g., the universal dignity and worth of human life). But even if the body politic elaborates particular legislation, civil law is not on that account merely a matter of public consensus. Law retains its divine origin and significance even where the public may not perceive this sanction. Obligation to conform to civil law does not depend upon public perception that God and the good are its ultimate foundation, although where this foundation is unperceived law loses much of its vitality.

Should either the left or the right impose morality by sheer power politics? Even if Christians were an absolute majority in society and the church could legislate against all sin, ought the church to do so? Some pornography, for example, is clearly vicious, some raises the question of legitimate art and is a matter of individual judgment, and some printed porn raises the further issue of freedom of the press. Should pornography be countered at the level of distribution or of publication or both?

In inferring particulars from general principles a variety of legislative options is possible, and not all differences in formulating alternatives are necessarily fallible. No less than changing majority views, changing cultures and times often require reviewing, revising, supplementing, or canceling particular statutes.

Many Christians are reluctant to engage in political affairs because they feel they should concern themselves only with changeless absolutes. But in a pluralistic society legislation is essentially a matter of compromise; in the absence of a clear majority consensus, the political outlook is shaped by coordinating coalitions that share common concerns.

Evangelical Political Commitments

Political commitments can become readily captive to principles or preferences alien to the church when evangelical movements align themselves uncritically with one specific political party and promote the election or defeat of candidates only on the basis of a highly selective agenda of legislation (e.g., anti-Panama Canal treaty, anti-SALT II) instead of working through all parties to promote a cluster of logically related commitments.

Some evangelicals contend that a proper concept of the church disallows Christian politicizing on either the left or the right. But in that event the lordship of Christ counts for little when a political movement opposes private property, for example, or promotes forced redistribution of wealth. Some options (e.g., totalitarian government, preservation of human rights including property rights) are issues on which a biblical faith has identifiable political implications. If the church is to be faithful in matters of biblical social ethics then Christians cannot be silent when political movements support issues or take sides in ways contrary to scriptural guidelines. Is the Christian witness only one of criticism and not of legitimating any alternatives? Christians are less than faithful to Christ's lordship over all political concerns if they imply that no moral choices flow from Christ's lordship in matters of political decision.

A clear conflict exists in the Christian community—even among evangelicals, including leaders of activist groups—on a number of important political issues. According to Professor Robert Webber of Wheaton College, nine out of ten professors of social ethics in evangelical colleges and seminaries hold views, as he does, akin to those of *Sojourners* magazine. Is that a fair reading of evangelical leadership in sociopolitical affairs? Moral Majority and Religious Roundtable contend, on the other hand, that the vast majority of evangelical Christians are firmly on the political right. What do these conflicting claims forbode for the future of the evangelical thrust in American national life? Jerry Falwell, who has emerged as the most prominent spokesperson for the fundamentalist right, has called for a coalition of conservatives on common objectives. Can evangelicals and fundamentalists forge a coalition of common political concerns instead of expending their energies mostly in internal conflict?

Promoting Evangelical Renewal and National Righteousness

The real unity of American life can be found only by a widespread recovery of common values and goals, and by a new regard for the God of justice and of justification. The present national crisis calls for a coalition that not only champions a new respect for life and law and property, but also reaffirms the transcendent authority of the living God and proclaims a dynamic for transforming inner attitudes and motivations and for voluntarily altering social behavior. If love becomes the heartbeat of the evangelical churches, if these churches are models of justice in society, if the new community of holy joy obtrudes as an exemplary human brotherhood and fellowship, if the biblically based churches can exhibit more fully in their own ranks the unity of the people of God, then they may be able, by open identification and involvement in community life, to stir the masses to an awakened voluntary interest in those vitalities essential to the soundness and stability of the political arena.

In the last analysis, a good society is one that seeks the good not because it is legally coerced to do so but because it is inwardly motivated. Christians cannot hope to reshape the world by political crusades; they must address attitudes and motives as well as structures. They do this most effectively when they speak of transformed humans whose perspectives Christ has changed and altered, and when they recognize in the mass media an effective bridge of communication by which the church can speak to secular society. Nowhere in the world do Christians have greater resources and freedoms to promote evangelical renewal and national righteousness than in the United States. But evangelicals will fail both the nation and their own heritage if they trust in political power to put America permanently on a course of moral leadership.

Unless the church proclaims the evangel to the multitudes, unless it disciples the nations and instructs the masses in all that Christ has commanded, unless it leaves no doubt to whom "all authority in heaven and on earth has been given" (Matthew 28:18), the church will forfeit its great and indispensable commission while it engages in the political realm only in a noble and necessary mission. If Christians ultimately fail, as well they may, in efforts to tilt the balance of civil authority from the beast-state (Revelation 13) toward that of a God-state (Romans 13), they will at least, like the early believers in Caesar's time, know and let it be known who is the Lord of history and the King of kings.

"The Evangel and Public Duty," Notes

1. John T. Noonan, Jr., *A Private Choice: Abortion in America in the Seventies* (New York: The Free Press, 1979), p. 192.

2. Lance Morrow, "What Is the Point of Working?" *Time*, 11 May 1981, pp. 93f.

3. Ernest Best, *The Letter of Paul to the Romans*, The Cambridge Bible Commentary (Cambridge: Cambridge University Press, 1967), p. 150.

4. John Hart Ely, *Democracy and Distrust: A Theory of Judicial Review* (Cambridge, Mass.: Harvard University Press, 1980), p. 60.

5. Ely, *Democracy and Distrust*, p. 50.

6. Ely, *Democracy and Distrust*, p. 52.

Evangelical Perspective on Political Decision

EVANGELICAL POLITICAL INVOLVEMENT: SOME DOUBTS ABOUT ITS EFFECTIVENESS

*T*he evangelical Christian challenges the currently normative mode of American politics. He does so, moreover, in a manner largely different from the radical Anabaptist tradition, which rejects direct political participation and encourages mostly negative criticism. While evangelicals emphasize the church's distinctive community witness within society as a whole, they also advocate direct political participation. They do not view political pursuit of the public good as mere rhetoric that cloaks private interests, nor do they consider the American political system as automatically suppressing Christian public concerns.

But despite their sense that American political processes can adequately reflect the common good, the evangelical community is increasingly apprehensive that the two major political parties, despite their differences, may through their presently shared policy

This essay was prepared August 1977 for the Inquiry into the Relationships between Religious Meaning and Political Action, a project of the Woodrow Wilson International Center for Scholars.

perspectives signal the need for a fundamental counterthrust. This evangelical dissatisfaction is not focused on the American Constitution nor on the established American political tradition, but increasingly questions the sanctity of the two party system, the growing power of vocal minorities, and the final authority even of majorities.

Despite the personal religious faith of many of the nation's political leaders, despite the public virtues still cherished by the grassroots citizenry, and despite the emphasis on representative pluralism which is declared to reflect national concerns comprehensively, the values traditionally considered normative in American society are now flouted with impugnity in many of the nation's influential and prestigious educational institutions, in the mass media, and even by some political leaders. Since the public good is unapologetically linked in evangelical political perception with ethical priorities, this trend nurtures doubts about the adequacy of present political processes to cope with the debilitating forces in American society. Every society postulates common convictions or values, and in their absence no political association either long retains stability or finally endures. The decreasing affirmation of inherited biblical values has nurtured an increasingly pragmatic, often unintegrated, and sometimes relativistic policy toward national values.

Whether obedience to God can be effectively expressed in the context of the burgeoning secular mindset in American society (e.g., current public school policy) raises mounting evangelical doubt that the present American political framework still constitutes a relatively just system within which Christian political expression is ideally possible. These doubts widen the sense of political alienation in the very decade in which the duty of political involvement is grasped as a Christian imperative.

THE IMPERATIVE OF POLITICAL INVOLVEMENT

Human Rights Endowed by God

Evangelical Christianity acknowledges God as Lord of the cosmos, of history, and of human life, and hence as the transcendent source, stipulator, and sanction of human responsibilities and rights. This emphasis is prominently reflected in the U.S. Declaration of Independence, which affirms that the human person is endowed by the Creator with certain inalienable rights. Civil government must preserve and protect these rights as a presupposition of its own legitimacy, and the citizen must live in responsible awareness that his or her rights terminate where those of a fellow citizen begin and that citizens have responsibilities to the government which maintains those rights.

Civil Government Established by God

The revealed will of God, published in the Judeo-Christian Scriptures, sanctions the role of civil government as the preserver of justice and promoter of social order and peace (Romans 13). This divine ideal will be enforced upon all the nations when the returning Messiah, Jesus Christ, reigns in power and glory. Its content is set forth in God's New Covenant, which embraces not only universal justice and harmony among the nations but the etching of the purposes of God upon the hearts of human beings; individuals and institutions thus fall under the searching scrutiny of God's holy will for man in society. The church as the New Society—a spiritually obedient vanguard of morally regenerate persons—is to mirror to the larger family of mankind the standards by which the returning Christ will judge human beings and the nations of the world. Yet the Christian shares also in this life in the present tragedy of rebellious human existence and is called to active participation in approving and advancing the divinely willed function of government.

All Human Activity Religious

The Christian concept of redemption anticipates the rescue of the penitent human person from the guilt, penalty, power, and presence of sin in all relationships, personal and societal. It anticipates that all rulers and nations will ultimately acknowledge Jesus Christ as King.

All human activity—political activity included—is religious, involving the human service of either the true God or of false gods. Every political proposal, decision, and act reflects underlying assumptions, however inexplicit. Every formulation presupposes a personal faith and public objectives. Politics is so far from being religiously neutral that Jacques Ellul has called it the modern man's god, the hopeful miracle worker trusted by the underprivileged for economic salvation.

The living God seeks in present history to advance only certain purposes through the church as a channel of redemptive grace and only certain purposes through civil government as the instrumentality of justice. There is therefore a sense in which the church is not to legislate sectarian religious objectives upon the nation as a whole, nor is civil government to coerce personal faith or to require or disallow what God requires or disallows. Yet the church has a proper eye to public conscience, virtue, and justice, and a rightful and necessary interest in the common good, while civil government is properly obliged to hold even voluntary religious associations answerable to just laws that are binding upon the body politic.

Public Policy Norms Provided by Scripture

God's New Covenant and principles of social ethics, both divinely revealed, supply the norms and criteria of public policy. The apostle Paul indicates that Christian and non-Christian alike stand in a relationship of conscientious submission to civil government in respect to public duties. The classic New Testament passage on civil responsibility (Romans 13) affirms that civil government has divine sanction to preserve public order for the social good, the good of Christians as well as others. The New Testament nowhere justifies anarchy. Rather it supports civil government as an institution, recognizing that at times particular governments may be tyrannical and even anti-God, suppressing good and rewarding evil (cf. the beast-state of Revelation 13).

The right of conscientious personal protest and disobedience is recognized, although the resister should be prepared to pay the legal penalties of civil disobedience. The fact that Paul calls the believer to submission (Romans 13:1, 5) rather than to unqualified obedience reflects the emphasis in Acts 5:29 that when civil government requires what is contrary to God's revealed will, it is God rather than men whom the Christian must obey.

DETERMINING ONE'S POLITICAL LOYALTIES

How then does the Christian decide whether disobedience to the governing authority is obligatory? Since the Christian political statesman seeks to sponsor and support just laws and to avoid impositions that might require citizens to act contrary to the will of God and to a good conscience, this question reflects also the larger query that seems currently so baffling to many persons: How in the wide range of public options does one discern the concrete proposals deserving of one's political loyalties?

Maintaining Biblical Perspective

The New Testament is not a book on ethical rules, although it does contain some rules ("pay your taxes," "pay just wages," "earn your pay"). Nor is it a book of political models. It does not approve any one form of government—whether monarchy, republic, or democracy—as ideal, although it does exclude tyranny. The New Testament assumes the legitimate existence of divergently formed nations. There is no single theological motif—whether the doctrine of creation, the Hebrew exodus, the Mosaic law (prophetic covenant and theocracy), the kingdom of God, Jesus' teaching and example, or the teaching and example of the apostles—from which answers to all questions about legislative specifics can be directly drawn.

The Bible supplies a theistic perspective, norms, principles, some examples, and a few rules. In view of these priorities, man in society is obliged everywhere to obey God and to love and serve him and his creatures. The Christian knows that he is redeemed by the mercy of God in Christ and is not in legalistic bondage to works; he seeks nonetheless through the enabling grace of the Holy Spirit to serve God obediently in gratitude for divine grace. The mandate of God's law and of universal justice and interpersonal love transcends that of obedience to all earthly authority. The claim that rulers make upon human beings must not annul the social commandments of the Decalogue ideally fulfilled in a spirit of neighbor-love irrespective of race, color, belief, or class. The very chapter in which the apostle Paul states human obligation to civil government states also that no claim must frustrate mutual love that fulfills the commandments of God:

> He who loves his fellow man has fulfilled the law. The commandments, "Do not commit adultery," "Do not murder," "Do not steal," "Do not covet," and whatever other commandment there may be, are summed up in this one rule: "Love your neighbor as yourself." Love does no harm to its neighbor. Therefore love is the fulfillment of the law (Romans 13:8-10).

The nation is therefore to be conceived first and foremost not as a world power, but as the servant of God in the righteous service of mankind at home and abroad. It places itself in the service of injustice when it accommodates or winks at adultery, murder, theft, and even covetousness, which rises readily from a confusion of human rights with human wants. The classic American political documents champion "the pursuit of happiness"; they do not promise or guarantee happiness or utopia.

Legislation that professes to be humanitarian while it lightens the seriousness of criminal offenses is a service neither to God nor to man. The primary purpose of punishment is not the reform of the offender but the vindication of the right and the peace and safety of society. A society that finds no basis for capital punishment (other than acts of terror made possible by twentieth century technology) retains only a shadow of biblical sensitivities to the worth of human life and readily elevates the value of the survival of criminals above that of their victims. Yet a compassionate interest in the prisoner (Matthew 25:36, 43) and a spirited concern for prison conditions belongs equally to the Christian social ethic and is specially imperative in view of the corruptive influence of many modern penal institutions.

Politics in Need of Clarity

It is therefore in respect to philosophy of law itself and the definition of justice that contemporary politics stands in dire need of clarity. In a day when predator powers pervert concepts of human rights and allow the totalitarian state to dictate what those rights will be, when they advance the forced redistribution of wealth as just, when they deplore political dissent as unjust, we must probe human rights anew in the context of transcendent foundations as distinct from political consensus. At the same time treaty signatories must be publicly commended or condemned for fidelity or nonfidelity to their United Nations Charter commitments.

While foreign policy must have in view international security and peace as commensurately important considerations, the advancing of human rights must be a forefront emphasis of any ethically sensitive international strategy. The arrest and imprisonment of citizens without public disclosure of charges, the use of torture methods to gain confessions, and the denial of prisoner contact with families and loved ones are marks of political irresponsibility that call for repudiation. Yet what is political convention in a particular historical context too readily and uncritically passes for a transcendent right.

A discussion of the nation's role as the servant of justice raises inevitably the problem of duties and treaty commitments to smaller powers. The temptation is to raise a moral umbrella over them only while they serve our national self-interest and later to abandon them in the game of power politics. In relation to Taiwan, for example, is it the course of justice to forsake that nation's right to independent sovereignty while we seek to improve relations with mainland China, even if we may no longer consider the Taiwanese government the sole legitimate voice of the mainland?

The principle of national servanthood requires something other than a permanent commitment to the notion of international power blocs that involve an escalating and unending arms race. To be sure, the presence of predator powers, whose shoddy historical record leaves little doubt of their ready takeover of weaker satellite countries, renders unwise a policy of unilateral disarmament. But any nation deeply disturbed about the perpetuation of nuclear rivalry will at the same time warn all human beings—those of predator powers as well as our own—what the present policy is doing to mankind.

Whatever are the requirements of a sound defense policy, the Christian task force is first and foremost on the side of world peace.

Only with deep indignation over international policies that impose these burdens upon the economy do Christians condone the vast military expenditures. In a time of widespread human poverty and opportunity for social betterment, these same moneys could help impart new dimensions of hope to the present social scene.

Hostility to communism is not the surest sign of competent foreign policy, for all the unconscionable communist repression of human liberty. The only adequate program consists in the sound promotion of freedom, of peace, of justice, of human decency and worth. In this cause we need to ally ourselves with voices for freedom and democracy that rise now and again within the communist sphere, reminding the masses that even Lenin held that a true socialist victory requires a context of political democracy.[1] We need to give political and mass media visibility to Solzhenitsyn and Sakharov, to keep in the public eye the names of victims of religious persecution such as Georgi Vins, to publicize underground repression of the Christian church in China and wherever else the ugly spectacle of spiritual persecution and intolerance remains. We need to admit our own national shortcomings and yet publicly celebrate progress made in preserving rights and invite the leaders of other lands to do the same—to reflect to the world the improving human rights record that bespeaks an ethically earnest society.

The noncommunist world yields too easily to the notion that Marxism has been the champion of human rights over property rights. But as a reaction to possibly valid Marxist criticism of economic wrongs, one need not espouse either an uncritical defense of secular capitalism or secular socialist alternatives. The failure of non-Marxist societies to engage in penetrating self-criticism should not lead us too readily to associate with supposedly ideal Marxist alternatives. The warped attempts to apply those alternatives give evidence that they are flawed in concept, and the crippling of the self-criticism process under Marxism should raise a flag of warning.

Political Priorities in Tension

If such broad emphases should commend themselves to all Christian statesmen, the fact remains that deep-seated differences or priorities in policy often vex political leaders of equally devout evangelical commitment. One major party may consider inflation a higher priority than employment while the other may consider employment a higher priority than inflation, at least for the near-term. There can be little doubt that ongoing inflation is a serious moral problem: it dissolves the worth of savings, discourages thrift on the part of any and all citizens, and erodes the purchasing power of wages. At the same time, the encouragement of ongoing welfare benefits without work and the breeding of a sense of personal worthlessness in the life of the unemployed worker whose energies could contribute constructively to the social whole, are harmful to the individual and to the nation. Hence a political situation in which both concerns are held in tension and kept in constant counterfocus as a target for solutions can be creatively served by leaders who opt for either priority.

The powerful role of labor unions, once so keenly necessary to avoid an exploitation of workers, now serves often to fuel the fires of inflation through rising wage and benefit demands indifferent to inflationary consequences. The time has come for political statesmen to realize that the inflation and unemployment crises are worsened through such demands, a fact officeholders are reluctant to challenge because they fear the loss of the labor movement's support. But the aggrandizement of personal power and private luxury by some labor leaders and their misuse of retirement funds have cost organized labor a diminution of enthusiastic support even within its own constituency.

Right-to-work laws are a test of the worker's liberty to gain employment simply on the basis of his abilities and the social need of his skills, and should not be opposed simply because organized labor seeks to extend its power and preferential position. The spirit of open competition needs to be nourished rather than depleted in the world of work, the more so when millions desire and need employment. The Bible teaches that human beings should normally be required to work in order to eat, and that means that maximal work opportunities are imperative. It is far better if voluntary agencies—business and industry, churches and service clubs, and other nongovernmental agencies—share this concern for man-as-worker than for government to add to its already staggering payroll by providing jobs for an otherwise unemployed citizenry. Government can sometimes serve employment concerns best by providing tax incentives to private initiatives rather than by becoming the rival of voluntary alternatives.

Before the American bicentennial, I proposed in a letter to the White House (promptly acknowledged and filed by a low-level correspondent) that the nation observe its two hundredth anniversary by encouraging every city and hamlet to undertake two civic projects: one to serve the majority and the other to serve the most neglected minority. I further proposed that these projects be accomplished by rallying business and service clubs and churches to work together with local government agencies to get the job done. Though nothing came of my recommendation, that spirit at the local level seems to me to be what America very much needs to capture, and the bicentennial could have served as a patriotic occasion to dramatize its merits as an ongoing frame of action.

Some word should be added about the growing disposition of government leaders to legalize gambling, a vice that encourages the notion that the best things in life can be acquired effortlessly; in fact it cheats most participants in order to favor a few. Such legalization is usually rationalized on the premises that it curtails the racketeers and produces government income. But the results are less impressive than anticipated on both counts, and the social cost of legalizing what is morally debatable and publicly harmful is high. There must be sounder ways to curtail the Mafia and to raise taxes than to get governments into the gambling business.

If government wishes to reward individuals, it would be far preferable to offer one million dollars annually for the best patented and marketed device that would serve such goals as energy conservation, food production, public safety, job expansion, and media breakthrough. Such a program would associate the hope of reward with creative contribution to the social good. And it would benefit the many.

Rising medical costs have crowded our country increasingly toward a national health insurance program. A costly cradle-to-the-grave program that promotes sound bodies while it destroys the economy is but a prelude to agony. The sense of social concern doubtless suggests the wisdom of catastrophic-sickness programs covering all citizens, not simply those with limited resources. Such a program should have specified limits so that it does not subsidize the unwarranted extension of the life of the terminally ill simply because of the availability of benefits. Moreover, the tendency to prey upon government funds in the name of the provision of health services, as in the case of Medicare abuses, should be discouraged by heavy penalties.

The issue of abortion is a highly sensitive and ethically important one. From its conception, the potentialities of the human fetus in the purpose of God puts a bold question mark over the morality of abortion-on-demand, the more so since society and its basic unit, the family itself, are involved. That abortion may be justified in relation to higher values—when the mother's life is threatened, for example, or in cases of incest and rape—is not disputed. But to reason that compassion requires destruction of the human fetus under circumstances of economic hardship is a specious syllogism even if some vocal church bodies sponsor it. There must be a better way to honor the desire not to have children than by officially accommodating the annual destruction of hundreds of thousands of fetuses.

Political Process as the Service of God

The lack of spiritual sensitivity and of moral consensus in American life has in recent decades largely been a reflection of three factors: the spiritual and moral ambiguity of the public schools and universities, the trend of the mass media, and the confusion in the American home (which in many respects reflects these influences). Insofar as American community life resists this tide of ethical relativism, the churches and spiritually conscientious families remain the major constructive influence.

But the founding fathers acknowledged religion and morality to be the twin supports of a worthy republic. (That by religion many if not most meant revealed religion is clear from the obvious fact that many other ancient religions accommodated ferocious totalitarian government.) The Constitution has, unfortunately, been widely misinterpreted as prohibiting the teaching of the Bible, even as literature and history, in the public schools. The recent trend has been to allow the nonestablishment clause of the First Amendment to erode much that rightfully remains under the rubric of individual freedom.

Congress can render few higher services than to call for an objective look at what the public schools and the media are doing to our generation, one in the name of a pluralistic society and the other in the name of commercial ratings. Such inquiry will doubtless be deplored as aimed at censorship, but if it exposes an implicit censorship posing as freedom, the cause of liberty will be well served.

Despite the boast that our nation affirms inalienable rights, few philosophy departments in our great public universities today espouse the supernatural theism on which the classic American political documents base their belief in divine creation and preservation of human dignity and worth. On the contrary, rival theories are ardently promoted. Yet only the balancing of human rights and duties on an objective transcendent basis will effectively challenge the modern isolation and fragmentation of rights (e.g., women's rights, black power, gay rights). The mass media are largely preoccupied with dramatic coverage of the colorful here-and-now aspects of the rights conflict and give inadequate attention to the governing philosophical and theological issues.

In the realm of legislative particulars, the political process deals with functional compromises of competing claims. The political statesman who seeks the ideal knows that he must cast his vote (if he is also a realist) for the best approximation of that ideal among the surviving options. He does so in humility born of an awareness that he too exists as a member of a finite and fallen society, and in confidence that despite his own limited insights he can rely on the operative providence of the God he serves. The laws that the Christian statesman sponsors are those he conscientiously considers better than rival options, yet he does not consider them unrevisable absolutes; the passing of years, sometimes only of months, may require a preferable alternative.

Politics is the obedient service of God in the midst of a changing and frequently unforseeable history. The norms and principles are fixed, and Christ at his return will demonstrate the superiority and durability of their uncompromised translation into history. In a society in which human beings remain free to mold their immediate political destiny, the principled politician will stimulate the conscience and will of his generation to reach as much as possible for the lasting good. The political leader has no calling to guarantee his own defeat at the polls; he is answerable to his constituency. But he serves his country and his God best—and his own constituency as well—if he risks all other claims in the promotion of what he confidently believes to be right and just. The scriptural norms and principles will function incomparably to identify the worthiest alternatives.

"Evangelical Perspective on Political Decision," Notes

1. Lenin, *On Socialist Democracy*.

The Crisis of our Times and Hope for Our Future

*T*he opening chapters of two great New Testament books keep running through my mind. Both deal with God's creation and its despoilment by sin; both hold out the alternatives of salvation or judgment. Both chapters are familiar to you, I'm sure. One is the classic prologue of John's Gospel; the other, that awesome first chapter of Paul's letter to the Romans.

John's prologue twice mentions darkness, each time sweepingly enough to cover not only man's fall and sinfulness but also the darkness of Crucifixion Day, and even that of our own declining civilization. How graphically this word "darkness" brings into focus the moral malignancy and spiritual sham of the human race! "The light shineth in darkness; and the darkness comprehended it not" (1:5, KJV). Other versions stress the point that no fury of darkness can overcome or extinguish God's light; until endtime judgment overtakes us, the light of God's living Word will continue to expose human wickedness for what it is.

This address was first presented on 14 May 1979 at the commencement exercises of Northwestern College (Reformed Church in America) in Orange City, Iowa. The college conferred on Dr. Henry an honorary doctorate in recognition of his theological, social, and evangelistic contribution in the world scene.

Romans chapter one is much more specific about moral evil. The exploding wickedness of the Gentile nations supplies a sort of Richter scale of civilizational decline, a measure of the slide of men and nations into the abyss of iniquity. As shocks and aftershocks of ethical earthquake surge over modern life, Paul's letter speaks not only to the Romans but to us also about the crucial crisis of our times, and the judgment that lowers above us.

The theme of Paul's epistle and of John's Gospel is the same: The light of God is shining through the darkness of human history and is penetrating the very mind and conscience of even a rebellious age. Suppress the truth of God though it may, fallen mankind can in no way eradicate it. God's light and truth remain and continue to unmask what we are.

THE PROCESS OF DECLINE

I spoke of a Richter scale of declining civilization. It works something like this. First there is a public awareness and retention of divine principles of righteousness; but alongside this awareness comes a growing public disposition to violate them. We have seen this in our own century. An earlier generation that was more largely aware of biblical and Christian roots conceded, for example, that God approves lifelong monogamous marriage and forbids extramarital sex.

Yet as society increasingly violates divine principles, such transgression soon becomes a matter of common practice and public acceptance. In our day sexual immorality outside marriage runs rampant. In some circles swapping mates has become almost a pastime, and for many young people marriages are made not in heaven but in hatchbacks and motels. Last year our country reported a million abortions, many of them the price of lust and immorality. Deterioration of the family is a recognized problem of modern society, yet many, including some clergymen, see abortion as a woman's right to avoid unwanted children and all too seldom emphasize the duty to uphold sexual fidelity.

Moral rebellion, the Bible warns us, runs a quickly accelerating course. When repeated compromise erodes God's norms of decency, respect for God soon yields to false gods that encourage sin and accommodate evil. God will permit a rebellious generation to suffer "the vileness of their own desires, and the consequent degradation of their bodies, because they have bartered away the true God for a false one" (Romans 1:24-25, NEB).

Refusal to honor God leads inevitably to destructive aftershocks: "thinking has ended in futility, and . . . misguided minds are plunged in darkness" (Romans 1:21, NEB). God gives them over, Scripture says, to "a base mind and to improper conduct" (Romans 1:28, RSV); to "their own irrational ideas and to their monstrous behavior" (JB); to a "reprobate" mind (KJV); to a "degenerate" mind (Phillips); to a "corrupted" mind (TEV); to a "depraved" mind (NIV). The Greek word *adokimos* identifies that which has failed the test. We too will fail the test unless with God's help we discipline our minds to follow Paul's challenge: "Whatever is true, whatever is noble, whatever is right, whatever is pure, whatever is lovely, whatever is admirable—if anything is excellent or praiseworthy—think about such things" (Philippians 4:8). Will we learn to think Christianly about the issues of life in the modern world?

THE IMPORTANCE OF THE MIND

The mind of man, as both John and Paul emphasize, is God's creation: by creation the Logos "gives light to every man" (John 1:9a), and despite our sinful state God's revelation penetrates our very mind and conscience (Romans 1:19-21; 2:15). Yet we read of mankind that "knowing God, they have refused to honour him as God, or to render him thanks" (Romans 1:21, NEB). The mind no less than the will of modern man is in dire trouble; having lost the meaning of meaning, our radically secular age cannot make up its mind about the truth. "That man should not think he will receive anything from the Lord; he is a double-minded man" (James 1:7-8).

We need to remember that the Bible links the moral decline of nations with reprobate minds. Training the mind is an essential responsibility of the home, the church, and the school. Unless evangelicals prod young people to disciplined thinking, they

waste—even undermine—one of Christianity's most precious resources. Leaders of the Protestant Reformation were all university
trained; they knew the Bible, the languages, philosophy, theology,
and much else. Secular liberal education today fails our generation
in the matter of consensus about either God or truth or moral
values. Many campuses seem unable to preserve respect for such
basic ethical virtues as repaying student loans, returning borrowed
library books, taking examinations or preparing term papers with
honesty.

MAN IN DEFECTION FROM GOD

Man's first step in defecting from God who makes known his
holy will is to replace the immortal God with mortal man (Romans
1:23). The ancients worshiped emperors, even their statues; mod-
erns worship the self as the measure of all things. This self-worship
is actually a divine judgment upon us for rejecting the one true
God. Such deliberate idolatry of the self quickly moves on to the
unbridled passion characteristic of our times. Paragons of permissive morality are welcomed as folk heroes to campuses, to television, and to the stage.

Who would have dreamed that the generation of the Billy
Graham crusades would also become the generation where many
champion homosexuality and lesbianism as no less moral than
heterosexuality and where others flee divinely created orders of
sexuality to become transvestites. If one has guilt feelings, there is
always some psychiatrist at hand to exorcise guilt.

We read of the ancient pagans that God at last "gave them
over to shameful lusts. Even their women exchanged natural relations for unnatural ones. In the same way the men also abandoned
natural relations with women and were inflamed with lust for one
another. Men committed indecent acts with other men" (Romans
1:26-27). In order to mirror the depth of inhuman perversion Paul
actually discards the Greek terms for "men" and "women" and
speaks instead of "males and females."

From a hit or miss consensus on values society quickly
moves to total disconsensus. "They have become filled," writes

Paul of earlier pagans, "with every kind of wickedness, evil, greed and depravity. They are full of envy, murder, strife, deceit and malice. They are . . . God-haters, insolent, arrogant and boastful; they invent ways of doing evil" (Romans 1:29-30). Reflect if you will on the ruthless violence of our own day: raping of helpless old women, raping of young wives, raping of teenage schoolchildren; street attacks on the elderly and the blind; senseless snipers that cut down innocent people; gruesome murders of young victims by sex maniacs. The stench of moral decay fouls the air as society is victimized by its own self-destructive vices. A new generation considers itself beyond fixed moral distinctions and indeed refuses to recognize them. Many academicians—both Marxist and non-Marxist—dismiss objective values as a prejudice of the establishment.

Small wonder that Soviet dissidents like Aleksandr Solzhenitsyn and Alexander Ginsburg, while finding grateful refuge among us from communist repression, nonetheless reserve the right to warn us concerning the moral flabbiness and vagabondage of the West. You and I know, of course, that much yet remains in America for which to thank God—not least of all, the freedom and opportunities envied by oppressed multitudes in many parts of the world. And we know that the day-to-day decency and good will of a multitude of God-fearing citizens seldom get the attention and headlines largely preempted by the seamy side of national life. We should be grateful that divine providence has gifted us with life in this land. President Jimmy Carter had every right to criticize a controlled society like Russia that seeks to seduce people "from God . . . through the television [and] through the schools."

But how much constructive influence do secular education and television in the free world actually wield for fixed truth and good in today's life of the people? The Russian social critics in our country seem to realize this peril better than we do. It is not enough to say that things are better in America than elsewhere; in every great world power that has marched off the map things once seemed better than anywhere else. Television encourages as its creed of modernity: "I believe in 'the way it is' according to Cronkite; in 'One Day at a Time' next week; and in 'Charlie's

Angels' in the life to come." Recently a special sale catalogue came in the mail from a large American publisher of college and university texts. Among the one thousand listings in philosophy, religion, politics, psychology, and other disciplines, only one title was premarked "sold out." What volume, you ask, was in such special academic demand? The title, believe it or not, was *Understanding the Female Orgasm*.

THE CONSEQUENCES OF OUR DECLINE

An impenitent generation, the apostle Paul tells us, "receives" its "due penalty," divine recompense proportionate to its own priorities. To suppress the knowledge of God will skew right and wrong with devastating final consequences. The fault line that opens our land to impending disaster seems increasingly to penetrate the very heart of modern culture. The tremors that presage God's final shaking of the earth reflect ever more blatant sin and indecency. Explosive forces are rumbling at the core of modern life; our civilization too may soon collapse into the same debris of human corruption that engulfed all past civilizations.

Amid the awesome prospects of a nuclear age, the Bible speaks almost apocalyptically of God's "meltdown" of his foes. Yahweh's warning against the sins of ancient Jerusalem should strike terror among today's rebellious nations that now rattle missiles instead of swords. Their horrendous unleashing of nature against mankind God despises: "As men gather silver, copper, iron, lead and tin into a furnace to melt it with a fiery blast, so will I gather you in my anger and my wrath and put you inside the city and melt you. I will gather you and I will blow on you with my fiery wrath, and you will be melted inside her. . . . and you will know that I the LORD have poured out my wrath upon you" (Ezekiel 22:20-22). Who of us can say that this nuclear generation is less worthy of God's terrible judgment than were Sodom and Gomorrah, Tyre and Sidon, disobedient Israel and Judah?

As a nation we have gone far beyond merely the neglect of God's moral principles to a routine violation of them. We have gone even further to outright rejection of those divine principles in the name of modernity. We are writing our own codes of right and wrong; man in place of God ventures to define the true and the good, and does so in the name of personal creativity and selfism. Today our nation is held together more by a network of governmental controls than by a shared consensus of values. Many of our universities have all but turned their backs on the Judeo-Christian heritage of revealed truth and divine commandments and have forsaken the pursuit of objective values. Are we as a nation encouraging and inviting the cataclysmic disaster that will plunge not only Western culture but all human history into final judgment?

GOD YET AT WORK

Even in the midst of this dark hour, the Christian community is called upon to sound the call of repentance, forgiveness, and God's triumph. God is still active in our secular society. He not only warns the impenitent masses of dire judgment but prods them also toward faith, and even prepares some for salvation. Multitudes today are thirsting for a personal faith. Many are looking for a messiah; they must be turned from false christs to the risen and returning Lord. God's Logos is still lighting every man, still shining in the darkness. The truth of God is still penetrating the mind and conscience of even the most wicked. Even some who seem hopelessly given over to iniquity may come by God's grace to new life and hope and joy. God is still at work in our world. He is manifesting the consequences of rebellion by abandoning the impenitent wicked to licentiousness and by allowing a long-privileged West to revert to paganism. But God is also lifting to his Savior Son those who seek refuge from the nihilism of daily life without Christ. In his mercy God enables even the desperate to embrace Christ as the rescuer from ruin and despair.

When Paul wrote his letter to the Romans this planet was overwhelmingly pagan. All the Christians to be found in the ancient empire city of Rome could have squeezed into a few small homes. But Paul knew something that, hopefully, you too know and will carry with you into a world desperately needing a vanguard of devout and dedicated disciples. Paul knew the reality and power of the Risen Christ who can turn a vagrant world right side up, can restore recognition of the Lord of nature, of history, and of conscience.

If hope is to prevail in our time, we who know God's transforming mercy and power must become roving tentmakers in the service of Christ who pitched his tent in a terribly wicked world and unveiled, for us to see, the glory of our life-renewing God. Let us call individuals and nations to a new vision of justice and righteousness. Let us invite a vagabond race to share with us the joys of life redeemed and fit for eternity. For the crisis of our times, the light that shines in darkness is still more than adequate.

Scripture Index

Subject Index